THE TUDOR DESPOTISM

THE MAKING OF THE
TUDOR DESPOTISM

by

C. H. Williams

*Professor of History in the
University of London*

NEW YORK / RUSSELL & RUSSELL

First published, November 1928
New edition, entirely revised and
reset, September 1935

REISSUED, 1967, BY RUSSELL & RUSSELL
A DIVISION OF ATHENEUM HOUSE, INC.
L. C. CATALOG CARD NO: 66−27183

PRINTED IN THE UNITED STATES OF AMERICA

AUTHOR'S NOTE

THIS book as originally planned was intended to attract the general reader as well as to cater for the student seeking a guide to the leading problems of early Tudor history. In preparing a new edition the author has kept this two-fold purpose in mind. The book has been in part modified, and the bibliography has been brought up-to-date. The main features remain as originally planned. In its new format it is hoped that the book will prove useful to a wider public.

The author wishes to express his thanks (without any imputation of responsibility) to Miss E. Jeffries Davis, Dr. H. W. Meikle, and Mr. C. G. Parsloe, for their kindness in reading this book, offering criticisms, and yet remaining his friends.

C. H. W.

King's College,
University of London,
July, 1935.

v

CONTENTS

THE MAKING OF THE
TUDOR DESPOTISM

CHAPTER I

BOSWORTH AND ITS IMPLICATIONS

THE deep significance of Bosworth will elude
us if we are content to view it as a battle in a
revolution. Its implications open on to subtler
problems, and the key to Henry's reign is a thorough appreciation of the spirit in which those
problems were met. Bosworth was not a battle
in the ordinary sense of the word. It was the
performance of a solemn ritual of mediæval law,
the testing of alleged legal rights by the familiar
process of ordeal by battle. From such a point
of view its vital feature was not that Henry Tudor
left the field alive, but that Richard III. remained
on it a naked corpse. For Henry's victory did
not mean that he had won a kingdom, but
Richard's death did mean for his contemporaries
a very solemn thing. It told them that however
slender might be Henry's legal right to govern
England, it was not as slender as that of one who
had been deserted by his God.

I

That Henry had a right to the crown he was not slow to assert long before Bosworth. It was, however, a questionable one, going back to Edward III. by way of Henry's mother, who was the granddaughter of an illegitimate son of John of Gaunt. Such a claim was not one to be pressed unduly, though it had its use, for it could be referred to when Henry wished to impress those Englishmen who liked to think, when they were in a fight, that they were on the side of God. It was, however, a less valuable argument than that which Bosworth Field provided, and it is in the consequences of Richard's death that the motives for Henry's immediate policy will be found. Some one must take Richard's place, and the divine judgment on the question of right enabled Henry to assert as dogma what had previously been mere hypothesis. In a word, Bosworth meant that the Tudor dynasty had been given its opportunity. Now that Richard was dead he could be pilloried as a usurper, and Henry could get a grip on the persons and possessions of those who had opposed him in the field. The work of government could be carried on. Royal estates and official positions could be distributed among friends. Control could be exercised over the treasury, customs could be collected, warrants could be issued, opponents could be crushed. Spectacular as all this appeared, it did not mean that Henry's position was secure, nor did it mean that England had been conquered. Until the verdict of the King of kings at Bosworth had been translated into the language of English law, Henry would continue to be a king, but a very special kind of king—a king *de facto*. Those tempted to pass this phrase unnoticed should pause to remember that it applies to kingship limitations similar in quality (though far more serious in results) to those intended by the War Office when it speaks of an officer as one who is " temporary and acting."

Three or four more months were to elapse before such a state of affairs could be changed, but the subtle nature of the achievement makes it worth attention, since it is at once the measure of the frailty and the strength of the foundations upon which the Tudor dynasty rested, and it is the first exhibition of a feature that we shall come to recognize as characteristic of all Tudor policy. In this first display of a reverence for legalism, an insistence on the strict letter of the law even in the most shady of undertakings and the most doubtful of actions, may be read the sign that a new dynasty has entered English history.

The process began with the summons of a parliament, and ended with the passing of an act ; but it is the intervening period that is really interesting, for it was during that time that Henry, like most men who fight, found himself in the hands of lawyers. The brief they had to argue was by no means a simple one. It was necessary for Henry to obtain a parliamentary title to the throne, but how could a parliament even consider the question of his rights since it must owe its very existence to the fact that Henry, as king, called it into being ? Indeed, how could it do

3

anything at all, for it was soon discovered that
many members had no standing in the parliament,
since they had been deprived of all civil rights by
acts of attainder passed against them in the time
of Richard III. Fortunately for Henry VII. and
for England, the lawyers of the fifteenth century
had become accustomed to settling such problems,
and if their solution lacks the beautiful precision
of a syllogism, it was at any rate based upon
sound common sense, and it could be put into
practice. They held that Henry, by picking up
the crown on Bosworth Field, had *ipso facto*
become king. Grant that assumption, and everything else follows quite logically. He could, as a
result of his kingship, summon a parliament. The
members who had been attainted must remain
outside the chamber until their colleagues had
passed acts to repeal those attainders, then they
could attend to their duties, and the real business
for which they had been summoned could begin.
Such advice was acted upon. Parliament proceeded to legislate about the king's title to the
crown. The act which embodied their ideas
merely declared that the inheritance of the crown
was, and should remain, in the most royal person
of the new sovereign lord, King Henry the
Seventh and his heirs. Parliament was very careful not to explain why, and we are thus left with
an ingenious solution of all difficulties by which
the decision of Bosworth Field was turned into
legal language without so much as a hint that
there had ever been such an episode as Bosworth
Field. Thus Henry became legally king of Eng-

land, not by conquest, not by hereditary right,
not by the election of parliament, but by a kind of
process of auto-suggestion which gave the impression that all three factors were of importance,
while all the time the real reason lay in the back-
ground. It was the very practical one that, for
the time being, there was no one in England who
was ready to tempt Providence as Richard had
done. Now, what had really happened was a
revolution, and to us it makes little difference
whether the events of 1485 are to be regarded as
a mere series of incidents, or as incidents clothed
in the forms of law. On the other hand it made
all the difference in the world to the man who had
been called by destiny to be the protagonist of
law and order, and whose conquest would only
remain unchallenged so long as he could argue
that there had never been a conquest.

All that had been done had been rendered
possible because of the death of Richard III.
Had that monarch lived on, even though defeated,
he would not have been a defeated man but a
defeated king, and in those circumstances the
element of conquest in Bosworth could not have
been so plausibly concealed. General support for
Henry would not by any means have been a
certainty. Richard's inevitable resistance might
have meant a fierce struggle, and in the end Henry
might have lost. These might-have-beens would
have followed the traditional sequence of fifteenth-
century history. They were buried once for all
in Richard's grave. All the consequences of his
death were not so advantageous to the founder of

the Tudor dynasty. Even though Richard could no longer lead a party, there was still a party to be led, and the means at its disposal for causing trouble were in reality more numerous with the late king out of the way. Pretenders could be found in all kinds of unlikely places and at all times. Their patched-up claims were obviously less defensible than Richard's would have been, but the element of mysterious fiction in which such claims were veiled made it no easy matter to disprove them. In considering Henry's reign, the long series of such adventurers must never be forgotten. They influenced his policy at every step. The rumours spread by Lord Lovell and Humphrey Stafford in 1486, to the effect that the real Earl of Warwick was in their keeping, might have brought disaster on the threshold of the reign had Henry not nonplussed them by acting very promptly. The imprudent schemes of an Oxford priest in 1487 resulted in Lambert Simnel's impersonation of Warwick, and caused Henry much anxiety until the motley army of continental adventurers and wild Irishmen had been beaten on the field of Stoke. Almost the only dramatic episode of the reign centres around Perkin Warbeck, the young man of mystery who seems to have been ready to believe that he was any one in the world save the son of a boatman from Tournai we think he really was. His romantic career as Richard of York cost Henry more anxiety than ought to fall to the lot of any monarch, during those years between 1491, when he first appeared in Ireland, and 1499, when he paid the penalty for presuming on the treatment Henry meted out to him after his exploits in Cornwall. " Henry," wrote a Spanish observer in 1499—when Ralph Wilford, son of a London cordwainer, was hanged for trying to turn into reality his dreams that he was a royal prince—" Henry has aged so much during the last two weeks that he seems to be twenty years older." It was not until 1500 that De Puebla was writing to his Spanish master to tell him that not a drop of doubtful royal blood then remained in the kingdom. And even after that Richard de la Pole was busy plotting trouble on the continent.

None of these adventurers, whose spasmodic intrigues won some measure of support in England, and whose schemes were planned or helped by Margaret, Duchess of Burgundy—the witch who never forgot that she was the sister of Edward IV.—could shake the Tudor throne ; but one after the other they formed a constant source of trouble to Henry, and probably they shaped his statecraft more than they could ever know. Their failures are the surest measure we can use whereby to estimate the full extent of Henry's policy in days to which the incidents of Bosworth Field were but the prelude.

CHAPTER II

LAW AND ORDER

NO man was less likely than Henry VII. to over-estimate the security to be expected from an act of parliament. To win the crown had been an easy task ; to keep it would be the difficulty, and for this something more would be required than reliance on the lip-service of an acquiescent parliament. To the solution of this problem Henry's activities had to be devoted during the greater part of his reign, and if we seek the permanent contribution of the first Tudor to the fortunes of his house, we shall do well to concentrate upon that policy of consolidation which resulted in the firm establishment upon the throne of a dynasty concerning whose legal claim to be there, perhaps the less said the better.

Henry's success in this work was very largely due to a reason that is not always remembered by those who deal with his reign. Henry was a mediæval man, and as such he might be expected to understand the problems common to all the centuries we sum up in the phrase the Middle Ages. Here is something worth attention, for whatever those who seek a clear-cut dividing line may say to the contrary, the whole of the fifteenth century—indeed, it is not extravagant to add a part of the sixteenth—belongs in spirit to the Middle Ages, and any attempt to mark the end of mediævalism by the battle of Bosworth fails, and well deserves to fail. That during this period indications were not wanting of a profound change in the outlook of men and in the characteristics of society, the succeeding pages will undoubtedly show, but that change must not be antedated, nor must the slowly dying past be hurried off the stage too soon. Justice will never be done to Henry VII., nor indeed to the Middle Ages, until the first Tudor king is taken out of what it pleases us to call the modern world and is put back into the mediæval surroundings in which alone he could feel quite at home. He was something better than a signpost pointing to the fields over which his son would one day walk. The qualities of statesmanship he showed were true to the traditions his noblest predecessors had bequeathed, and in him the Middle Ages found a monarch aiming at ideals that its greatest men had tried to reach. To end the mediæval period in the dismal chaos of a civil war is to rob those centuries of their unity. The reign of Henry VII. is not the beginning of modern times. It is the happy ending to the story of mediæval England.

The fifteenth century was, for the most part, a period of trial and troubles. It was not the first period of that kind in mediæval history, and the point would not be worth much notice were it not that with the similarity there was a difference. For much of the trouble was due to the impending collapse of the structure on which mediæval society rested. The signs of such a collapse were as yet indistinct, the main structure was still firm, but most of Henry VII.'s difficulties will be revealed to us if we give a quick glance to those beams on which the chief weight was falling.

The century opened with the most typical of mediæval adventures—a war of aggression with France. There were moments when the dream of an English empire in Europe looked as though it might be achieved, but the moments passed. All that this country acquired was a number of political and economic problems common to all wars, and peace dawned on a land where profiteers, militarists, unemployed, and taxpayers settled down together to live as best they could. It was unfortunate that at such a crisis there was no monarch strong enough to take full control, and for the rest of the century, at the moments when each ruler dropped the crown, might took precedence over right, and dignity was forgotten in a wild rush for possession. Symbolic is the story which tells that Henry VII. picked up the crown from under a thorn-bush after Bosworth had been fought. Mediæval political theorists had regarded the kingship as a breakwater against the restless sea of baronial faction, but the collapse of the kingship had let in flood tides. Faction raised against faction their petty pretenders to the throne, and the representatives of heaven became the puppets of kingmakers. The wars of the roses, a series of purposeless, destructive, and spasmodic battles, gave England years of uncertainty and a host of problems. While the greater part of the population went on with its work, a band of nobles turned the country into a tournament ground, and let loose evils with which the student of Tudor history must make himself familiar. Baronial feuds called into action soldiers trained in the French wars. They were retained for service by the lords, wore their masters' liveries, and made themselves the terror of the countryside. They were responsible for that " lack of governance " which left the statesman helpless. While their masters were busy sapping the earthworks of the central government, they were just as strenuously engaged in destroying that system of local government which had been the permanent contribution of the Middle Ages to the science of politics. When they broke the law they went unpunished, for their lords were either the justices of the peace before whom they were arraigned, or else they had sufficient influence with those in authority to modify their punishment so that it became no better than a mockery. Sheriffs dared not take action against them for fear of the reprisals that would follow. They were the terror of the juryman's life. It is hardly to be wondered at that in such circumstances the administration of law faltered, and the machinery of government broke down. Not that law ceased entirely to be administered. On the contrary, the most sinister feature of the period was the tendency for law itself to become the tool of lawlessness. The prevalence of corruption, intimidation, and the other abuses indicated above, often made it possible for the law itself to be used by powerful men against their weaker neighbours. No man with any considerable property dared to be without a knowledge of the law, for enemies at any moment might try to trick him out of his possessions by bringing false actions against him. It is little wonder that such conditions brought the England of the first three-quarters of the fifteenth century to a state which some writers have not hesitated to describe as little better than anarchy —though this is far too extreme a view—and that men of all conditions longed fervently for the restoration of strong government and peace. The strong government promised at the accession of Edward IV. and Richard III. was welcomed in the hope that it would achieve the desired result. The failure of both those monarchs gave Henry his opportunity.

The obvious path for him to take was that which would lead him back to the mediæval ideal of good government. A strong kingship, exercising absolute control over feudalism, must be established ; the disintegrating influence of the great lords must be destroyed. Efficient government, peace, and the maintenance of law and order were the objects that must be attained. It is wrong to regard such a policy as revolutionary, or a peculiarly modern contribution to the problem of government. It had been the ideal of Edward I., and before him of Henry II. That the strong kingship to which it would lead would have some of the characteristics of despotism was inevitable. All mediæval attempts to enforce such a policy had tended in such a direction. That it was to lead to a *Tudor* despotism was due to the working of forces that Henry himself could not have conceived.

Henry's problems are best epitomized by an incident of the first year of his reign. The judges held a meeting to discuss the legislation that was to be drafted for consideration in the first parliament. Many proposals for statutes were brought forward, but one judge brushed aside all such suggestions with the remark that there were plenty of acts of parliament in existence. What was wanted was not fresh legislation, but some method whereby existing laws could be enforced. Henry's task was to supply that method. He came to fulfil the mediæval law. The spirit which pervades all his statutes is mediæval : but for once the mediæval disparity between legislative theory and practice was about to be considerably modified.

Three main ideals form the basis of Henry's policy. His supreme objective was the consolidation of his own kingship. All he did was done to strengthen his own position and justify the support he had received in the country. This could only be done by achieving his second ideal, the restoration of the rule of law. Men expected his reign to fulfil their hopes of peace by bringing chronic lawlessness to an end, and Henry determined that this should be done. Such hopes could only materialize if law itself was made attractive. The establishment of an efficient administration was the third object of his work.

The consolidation of his own position entailed severe action against the turbulent aristocracy, for until the baronial opposition had been rendered innocuous there could be no hope of peace. His first act for this purpose was a gesture of reconciliation. On January 18, 1486, he married Elizabeth of York. That Henry intended the marriage to influence his claim to the throne is doubtful; that he meant it to ensure the claim of any heir of his is certain. For this alliance defeated the anarchical policy of the nobility by taking away from them the cause of party division, and the union of the roses destroyed for ever the pretext of the wars of the roses. The suicidal results of those feuds in the past, coupled with the decay of the structure of feudal society, had weakened the baronial opposition, so that Henry's attack upon what strength still remained to the nobles could be made with little risk. The English ruling families could be, and were, ignored. Henry relied for assistance and advice upon " new men."

The weakened baronage was rendered innocuous by a systematic insistence upon the rule of law which deprived its members of the assistance of their retainers. The armed camps of fighting men were broken up by the enforcement of laws against maintenance and livery, the dangers of intimidation were checked by severe penalties levelled against those responsible for gathering together unlawful assemblies of people, and riots were followed by heavy punishments on offenders. An attempt was made to remove the temptation to lawlessness by exterminating its agents, and

the attempt was largely successful. Discretion
marked the working out of Henry's schemes.
The rebellions of the reign were a challenge to the
new order, but the spirit in which they were met
was always the same. From Stafford's rising, in
1486, to the demonstrations in favour of Perkin
Warbeck, the end can always be foretold. Ring-
leaders were ruthlessly dealt with, but the rank
and file were silenced by the sight of the majesty
of the law, and pardons were lavishly issued on
payment of fines.

Insistence on the rule of law was not enough.
The administration of law had to be so improved
as to make it popular. Much active work was
done in this direction, and a policy was evolved
which attempted to deal with the two problems
that had to be solved. In the first place, there
could be no rule of law without an efficient system
of legal administration. In the second place, the
working of the machinery of law had to be made
so smooth that it could be set in motion easily
and in any circumstances. The legal machine had
to be able to check the overmighty subject as well
as the petty offender, and, conversely, it had to
be such as could be used in the interests of the
poorest, least influential member of society, as
well as in those of the rich and of those who were
learned in the law. The solution of the first of
these problems was detailed overhauling of the
whole administrative system. Corrupt officials
who stood in the way of efficiency were dismissed,
and penalties were fixed for those who should
transgress in the future. Statutes defined the

duties of sheriffs, coroners, justices of the peace, and other local officials, and a tariff of fines and heavier penalties were fixed for the neglect of such work. The jury system, which had almost broken down under the weight of systematic intimidation and bribery brought to bear upon it, was restored to working order by penalties for false verdicts, punishments for perjury, and rigid control over the jurors. Finally, the legal procedure, which had grown somewhat obsolete through rigid adherence to stereotyped forms, was brought more up-to-date by attempts to expedite the hearing of cases and the punishment of crime. Much still remained to be done in this direction after Henry had finished his work, for legal procedure still retained many of its mediæval abuses until well into modern times ; but Henry at least did his best to remedy some of the more crying abuses.

This serious attempt at the reform of the local administration of justice was essential, because it robbed the nobles of their greatest source of strength by establishing firm control over the country-side where they had terrorized their inferiors. But before the full effects of the new system could be felt, it had to provide remedies within the reach of all subjects without distinction of class or power, and to this end important reorganization had to be carried out at the centre of government. The reform of the local administration was supported by equally drastic changes in the organization of central government. Their purpose was to make possible the exercise of a full control over those elements in the country whose efforts were directed to the obstruction of the reforms in progress. The overmighty subject, the offenders against the new system—such as jurymen guilty of perjury, or men who refused to obey the rulings of inferior courts—had to be brought below the law. For this purpose the old idea of a control exercised by the king's council over all branches of the common law was adapted to meet new needs. Strengthened by exercise, the judicial functions of the council were developed into an organ of government, and in the star chamber there was established a judicial body which was to become an important feature of Tudor government. Modern scholarship has given much attention to the problem of the origins of this court, and a great deal has been said which goes to prove that the simple theory tracing it to an act of 1487 is not a satisfactory explanation. Research has shown that the act in question, although called the Star Chamber Act, in reality does not mention the words star chamber, which are only an interpolation of a later date. Thus the act is one which makes provision for some form of jurisdiction outside the common law to deal with offences like maintenance which were such a serious menace to peace. To regard it as the means whereby the court of star chamber was called into existence is to forget that the mediæval council had always possessed a special jurisdiction above the common law. It is this special jurisdiction exercised by the council in the star chamber long before 1487 which is the real basis of the court of star chamber. In relation to this conciliar jurisdiction the act of 1487 must be regarded as a minor regulation chiefly important because it reveals Henry applying some of the powers of the mediæval council to special purposes. The arguments connected with this problem are far too complicated to be dealt with here, but the conclusion to which they lead is of value to the student of Henry's policy. That conclusion is yet another proof of the logic of the first Tudor's schemes. For Henry's policy was not revolutionary in the way in which it would appear to be if the court of star chamber were really a creation of an act in 1487. What he was doing in those early years of his reign was wholly in keeping with his policy of fulfilling mediæval ideals. He was restoring the judicial functions of the mediæval council by giving that body more work to do, and gradually—so gradually that it is impossible to fix the date for it—the judicial work of the council became so important that men spoke of it as being done in and by the court of star chamber. Certainly before the reign was ended such a court had become a powerful agent of the new government. It was in a stronger position than the common law courts to deal with the difficult problems of law which were raised by the existence of the overmighty subject. The new court was not hampered by the forms or the formalism of the common law courts. It could act promptly, had a different kind of procedure, and was able to draw on the reserve forces of the central government in a way quite impossible for the older courts. It was therefore able to enforce

its punishments and compel justice to take its
course against those who were too strong to be
dealt with in the ordinary way. For the court of
star chamber was reserved the work of dealing
with those difficult problems which could not be
settled in courts with less authority.

If the proceedings in the star chamber be
examined, it will be found that the cases heard
there were cases which concerned both poor and
rich. There were cases in which overmighty
subjects were being proceeded against in the
interests of poor suitors who would otherwise
have been powerless against them. There were
others in which the state was taking care of its
own interests, because the offenders were breaking
the laws which it had specially enacted against
those who took the law into their own hands.
Most of the court's time was taken up with the
hearing of petitions from poor persons who had
been unjustly deprived of their possessions or had
been subjected to the lawless treatment familiar to
the fifteenth century, but difficult to remedy in
the ordinary courts of law. And side by side with
those cases were heard those in which defendants
were guilty of serious breaches of statutes against
maintenance and livery and other acts aimed at
the suppression of lawlessness. In a word, any
case which was not easy to settle in the ordinary
courts, because of the activity of the vested interests against which the government was making
its stand, could be brought into the star chamber,
where there was more than a hope that it would
be effectively dispatched. The court of star

chamber was to succeed by success. Its value to the crown was speedily recognized. Under the guidance of Wolsey it was given more work to do, and for the rest of the Tudor period it was to remain a symbol of the ideals and the resources of the new monarchy. Like most institutions that men devise, the court of star chamber was to become a power too easily abused by unscrupulous rulers, and its value to the government turned it into a menace to the community. In the days of Henry VII. such a calamity could scarcely be foreseen. The court was in its infancy, and there lay before it many years in which the work it did was for the most part good.

Such were some of the expedients which made possible a check upon the general lawlessness prevalent throughout the country ; but no account of the machinery of government constructed by Henry's tireless efforts would give the reasons for his success unless something was said of the policy applied to the working of the central administration. Here, too, the problems before the new king were numerous, though all of one kind. For the menace to any efficient system of government was the nobility, and if Henry was to be master in his own kingdom he must provide a system which would be worked independently of the great lords, since their activities would always be directed towards stimulating feuds and circumventing the measures that were being taken against them and their supporters. Henry met their threat by dispensing with their help. This was done by refurbishing the agent of government which had seen much service in mediæval times, and whose potentialities for good had been foretold by a keen political theorist of the fifteenth century. Though it would be hard to prove that Henry was consciously imitating the theories worked out in Chief Justice Fortescue's book on the *Governance of England*, which was written between the years 1471 and 1476, there can be little doubt that all his work would have met with the complete approval of that worldly-wise lawyer. Probably the truth is that Henry's immediate predecessors, Edward IV. and Richard III., had attempted to put into practice the ideas of Fortescue, and that Henry simply developed their work. Whether that be so or not, Henry realized that the solution of his problems lay along lines mapped out by Fortescue. Like the lawyer, Henry saw the possibilities inherent in the mediæval council, and in the structure and use of such a body lies a great part of his contribution to the establishment of efficient government. In dealing with Henry's advisory body we are, unfortunately, studying an organization about which we know very little, save the positive and lamentable fact that its records have been almost wholly lost. We know enough, however, to see the ideas underlying it, and the possibility of further development which these ideas implied. It was, from the beginning, a somewhat nebulous institution, constructed for use rather than for ornament, and its personnel was therefore deliberately left a little vague. Henry's purpose was to break away from the past by methods earlier kings had occasionally tried, but he was to extend their ideas in a way of which none of them had ever dreamed. Instead of calling to his councils the nobles who regarded it as their right to be present, he struck out on bold lines. His council consisted of any one whom the king wished to call in for advice, and the nucleus of his advisers consisted of a band of men who owed to the king their positions and all their hopes of promotion. Instead of the historic names of the English peerage that make up the lists of counsellors in earlier reigns, the prominent names in Henry's council are those of worthy but comparatively unknown and unimportant men like Bray, Cheyney, Conway, Dudley, Dynham, Empson, Fox, and others. The change is one to be noticed very carefully. In part it is an eloquent comment on the feuds of the roses, which had robbed so many noble houses of their heads ; but it is in greater part the sign of Henry's new régime. For it means that the control of government and policy had been put entirely into the hands of the king himself, since these new counsellors owed all to their royal master. The body in which such men were prominent was hardly likely to be obstinately opposed to the wishes of the king. It existed in order to carry out his policy. There follows, too, another truth. Since this body was subservient, it inevitably took a greater part in the work of government than a more independent council would have done. Henry knew that his council could be trusted to work in harmony with him, so he was never afraid to give it work to do, and as a result the council went on increasing in importance as it proved its usefulness. What part it was finally to play will best be seen when we have been able to watch it at work in later times, for with the growth of its importance there went an increase in its records, and it is easier to glean an impression of its activities when these are available for study. For the present it is sufficient to notice that it was under Henry VII. that the activity of the council began. An effective instrument had been placed in the hands of a king whose energy was devoted to the task of making government efficient.

By all these means a strong central government in the control of the king was able to supervise the activities of local officials, putting into operation the policy that was clearly defined in Henry's mind. In such circumstances the end of lawlessness could only be a question of time. The attainment of Henry's main objective—the consolidation of his own position—seemed to be at hand.

It could not be fully achieved without serious attention to another problem. All good government is, in the last resort, a matter of money, and if Henry's ideals were to be realized they would have to be financed. The depletion of the treasury during the chaos of the civil wars was only too evident. If Henry was to replenish his resources, a ruthless financial policy would be necessary. The undertaking was one that might well be dreaded by any monarch whose position was as uncertain as Henry's was, for the reformer is only popular until it is time to pay for his schemes.

23

Even here Henry's characteristic caution prevailed. If his financial policy be examined, it will be found to be divided by a date which roughly coincides with the period when he was beginning to feel safe from the plots of usurpers. That dividing line may be drawn somewhere about 1500. In the years before that date Henry's plan was to make the most of what he had. After that date he became less scrupulous, more daring in his financial experiments. The first period saw the king resuming possession of crown lands which had been alienated in reckless generosity by his predecessors, and adding to this source of income by ruthless accumulation of lands escheated to the crown by the attainders of their owners. Skilful use was made of the feudal incidents, wardships, reliefs, and feudal aids, while a parliamentary grant of tonnage and poundage for life added another source of revenue. Expenditure was a greater problem than revenue. Economy was practised on a large scale. In the first parliament of the reign an elaborate scheme was prepared whereby a fixed sum of money was set aside for the expenses of the royal household, and an attempt was made to live within these limits by the keeping of most detailed accounts. Even the king's pocket money was carefully accounted for, with the result that we are in possession of the merest details of his daily expenditure. Such reforms did something to check the extravagance common in earlier reigns, and the thrift which they inculcated soon had an effect on the treasury. They have also left their mark on the history of the reign, for the

24

description of Henry as a miser is largely the result of generalizations based on the knowledge that he kept such careful accounts. The verdict is not altogether fair to him. Henry was careful rather than miserly. He spent lavishly on himself and his household, paid his many gambling debts like a gentleman, and his wife's debts like a model husband. He spent a great deal in almsgiving, was a generous patron to the arts, and laid out large sums on building. The huge amounts he was continually spending on jewellery represented sound business policy rather than childish extravagance. In an age when credit was not easily obtained at the psychological moment, a well-filled treasury was indispensable, and the coffers which Henry bequeathed to his son were not the accumulation of a miser so much as the safeguard of a king who knew how impossible it was to rule without resources. The story of Henry's financial policy must not be taken up entirely with eulogy. There are ugly traits to be emphasized. His financial transactions were not all above reproach. In the second period, after 1500, there can be traced the sinister signs of a less scrupulous policy in money matters. Not only were the older sources of supply still drawn upon, but newer and less reputable methods of adding to revenue were coming into use. By means of forced loans, the practice of selling honours that is concealed in the phrase " distraint of knighthood," the use of legal procedure in order to force unfortunate individuals to give up their wealth, and by other forms of disreputable trickery, the king's agents fulfilled the royal wish for a full treasury. The change speaks volumes for Henry's constitutional achievements. A king must be in a very safe position, with the government of the country well in his control, before he dares to risk the danger of rousing his subjects by questionable methods of emptying their pockets.

That, when all is said, is the final comment to be made on Henry's statecraft. He came to the throne of England an untried adventurer, and he made good. When the time came for him to lay aside the sceptre he was the father of a dynasty, and a new epoch had opened in English history. The work he did was not spectacular, but it was indispensable. He brought England peace, and made possible the rule of law. If he had done nothing else, his work would still be great enough to win for him a high place in Tudor—and in English—history. But it was not all. The gradual consolidation that he achieved by putting into operation the policy we have but sketched, was work which occupied his time and drained his energies throughout the better part of his reign. It did not blind him to the fact that he had other work to do. It was work we shall not understand until we have realized that England was not Europe.

CHAPTER III

THE period of the wars of the roses had not been lacking in contact between English statesmen and the diplomatists of the European world, but the interests of foreigners had been concentrated upon the struggle going on within this country. Their activities usually took the form of open or secret intervention on the side of one or other of the parties, in order to ensure the continuation of the chaos so as to prevent English activity in continental affairs.

It was for this reason that Henry VII. was forced to pay attention to foreign policy. Circumstances over which he had no control compelled him to take up the challenge of other nations. He had to become a diplomatist in order to remain a king, for the very zeal with which he devoted his attention to domestic affairs, and the consolidation of his own position at home, drew him inevitably into the whirlpool of continental politics. The paradox of his foreign policy lies in the thought that the less he interfered in European affairs the more important he and his country became. What he had to do was to withdraw English affairs from the prying eyes and meddling fingers of foreign diplomats, and straightway he made England a centre of attraction for all the chancelleries of Europe. It was a novel policy, and it succeeded. Some of the more important of its results did not come until after Henry's days were done, but this should not be allowed to prejudice his claims to credit for the advantages which ultimately accrued, nor—let it be added in passing—should it absolve him from responsibility for some of the less fortunate results of the policy which he initiated. He had his share in the good and evil which later events were to bring to this country. The day would dawn when the little island, which to all intents and purposes was in Henry's time an outpost at the end of the world, would become the power in whose keeping lay the fortunes of a great part of Europe, and even Henry's immediate successor would be able to play no small part in the working out of continental politics. These eventualities were in great measure the work of Henry's successors, but his own share in the creation of the factors making such eventualities possible must be taken into account in an analysis of the work done during his reign.

To follow the course of Henry's schemes, we must approach them with minds freed from some familiar ideas. First and foremost it is essential to reject the standards by which diplomatic work is too often judged, and instead of pursuing the conventional path of praising Henry as a great foreign minister by ascribing to him actions he neither did nor intended to do, we must centre attention upon, and give him credit for, what he did not do rather than for what he did. The accepted tests will not avail. If the success of foreign policy is to be sought in conventional signs, the result of Henry's work will prove disappointing. In his schemes there were no dazzling military expeditions, no plans for the realization of imperial dreams, no ringing challenges to stir the enthusiasms of his subjects and bring fear to his foes. His foreign policy was one of pen and ink rather than of blood and iron, and his victories will be found hidden amongst the state papers existing for his reign, rather than on fields of battle. Even in such paper warfare Henry was not uniformly successful. Contemporaries were not always duped ; Henry did not invariably get his way. And yet, despite the lack of show, allowing, too, for the unattractive features of much of his policy, something was being accomplished to which generosity will not grudge the name success. Much depends on the standards adopted for the criticism of his work. If we judge by show, we shall find it hard to make a case for Henry. If, on the other hand, the problem be approached from another angle, we shall find that this unheroic, unspectacular policy was at once the cause and the explanation of much which must otherwise remain a bewildering feature of sixteenth-century history. To reach that angle, however, we must sacrifice another familiar idea. To realize England as a foreign power during this period, we must first of all learn to forget England.

The mind accustomed to look upon European history from the English side of the Channel has little hope of being able to grasp firmly the prob-

lems of sixteenth-century history, and still less
chance of catching the meaning of early Tudor
policy. For the theme of English history during
the greater part of the sixteenth century is the
steady change in the status of England in the eyes
of Europeans. Provided that too literal an interpretation be not placed upon the analogy, that
change may be roughly described as one whereby
England underwent a transformation on the
European chessboard. At the opening of the
Tudor period England's representative was a pawn
able to move in the narrow limits prescribed for
that piece. By the end of the period the pawn had
become a queen, able to move in all directions and
apt to upset all the traditional and preconceived
notions of continental statesmen by the unex-
pectedness of some of the moves she made. We
are here concerned with the pawn, and our task
must be to take up a position somewhere in Europe
where we may realize to the full how unimportant
England was in the years when Henry VII. first
took control of her fortunes.

No better vantage-ground for such a survey of
the European scene can be imagined than the
highest point in Christendom, St. Peter's throne
at Rome. Its occupant had every incentive to
make himself familiar with the political landscape.
As head of a Church whose complex organization
embraced the whole of the European world, it was
his business to know everything going on in the
world around him, and in the difficult times in
which he lived Pope Innocent VIII. (1484-92)
had reason to follow such transactions very closely.

He ruled at a critical point in the history of
the Church, at a time when that institution—
chastened, though not depressed after the disgraceful episode of the Babylonish Captivity—
was beginning to reap some of the rewards of the
period of good resolutions and reforms which
followed the attempts of the Conciliar Movement
to put the temple in order. The Papacy was
trying to win back some of its lost prestige and
power, and by a steady policy of consolidation
was seeking to strengthen itself financially and
politically.

There were some indications that success might
be achieved. From its age-old rival the Empire,
the Papacy had little to fear. The temporal power
had lost the virility with which it had time and
again thrown out a challenge to claims of papal
supremacy. The emperor had become a ghostly
shadow ; his dominions were the prey of a disintegrating feudalism which was dragging them
down to anarchy. Lawlessness, private warfare,
and the separatist ambitions of the princes had
reduced the emperor to impotence, and the long-
drawn struggle between him and his feudal inferiors hindered the working out of any logical
imperial policy. Frederick III. (1440–93), slow-
moving, building for the future while he was losing
what he had, and Maximilian (1493–1519), the
shifty adventurer whom only he himself took
seriously—these were not dangerous rivals. From
the Empire under such rulers there was very little
for the Papacy to fear.

The real problems of papal and European

politics lay elsewhere, and they were not to be so lightly put on one side. By the last quarter of the fifteenth century the sinister results of the new methods in papal policy were revealing themselves, and the sight was not a reassuring one for the head of the Church. What those results meant will be clear when it is remembered that with the accession of Sixtus IV. (1471–84) the Papacy entered upon a period when worldly interests were paramount in the minds of those guiding the Church. The lowered moral tone Sixtus introduced into ecclesiastical policy was not likely to work for the advantage of an institution whose special charge was the spiritual welfare of the world. The Great Schism (1378–1417) had caused a weakening of papal power, and in his efforts to win back strength, Sixtus fixed his hopes on the consolidation of the temporal power of the Papacy. The objective towards which he worked was the more complete control of the papal patrimony, and his energies were directed towards the extension of those dominions for the additional wealth and prestige in Italy that such additions would bring. It was a dangerous policy, and the dangers were not long in making themselves felt. The Papacy became increasingly involved in the affairs of this world. In a little while the head of a Church, whose claims to universal respect had been the insistent catholicity of his claims, sank to the level of a petty Italian prince busied with the parochialism of Italian politics.

The decline was not wholly due to the work of Sixtus, for it was accompanied by a moral degeneration which was largely the result of the awakening intellectual enthusiasm of the renaissance age. The assistance given by the Papacy in the fifteenth century to the revived enthusiasm for learning cannot be denied; but the gain of the world was in part loss to the Church. Classicism, pagan culture, critical study of the classic texts, and the new standards of taste following these activities, reacted upon the minds of the leaders of the Church, and the example set by the renaissance popes was not likely to win back from the European nations the respect forfeited earlier in the fifteenth century. That period had wrought irreparable damage. As a result of it, the rapidly awakening nation states of Europe were beginning to press their claims more heavily in opposition to the traditional privileges of the Church. They were claims which cut to the roots of papal theory and practice. In France, Spain, and England a more or less violent assault was being made upon the foundations of papal organization. The civil power in these states was feeling its way towards a policy of independence. Jealous for its own prestige, the state was everywhere beginning to translate into action its claim to a share, at any rate, of the control exercised by the Church in the administration of church offices and benefices within the boundaries of the respective nations. Eager to strengthen its own position, the temporal power was casting jealous eyes upon the ecclesiastical revenues which yearly left the nation states for Rome. The policy which gave expression to such claims was more clearly defined in some states than it was in others, but wherever it was finding its voice it derived considerable advantage from the evil consequences of the demoralization which marked the Papacy. It would be easy to follow into much greater detail the signs pointing in the direction of the growth of this independent attitude towards Rome, but it would lead us away from the main subject in hand, and in so far as the tendency was to have an influence on the course of English history it will have to be treated at greater length in a later chapter. For the present we may content ourselves with one illustration of the significance of this new attitude towards Rome. The menace of a Turkish advance into Europe— with all the implications such an advance would mean—had touched the heart and the imagination of the European world on more than one occasion during the Middle Ages. The menace had never been more ominous, the chances of Turkish success rarely more auspicious, than after the fall of Constantinople in 1453. And yet, the prestige of the Papacy had fallen so low that in the late fifteenth and early sixteenth centuries the Pope had not moral authority enough to rally to his side a crusading army to beat back the attack. Not even Henry VII. could be roused by such a call to anything more than a politely worded refusal, and Henry was by no means the most aggressively anti-papal monarch of his day. That apathy is eloquent testimony of the steady decline in the moral prestige of the Papacy.

Such decline was not the only, not even the most important, factor in European politics during this period. If there was decline, there were also manifold signs of new life stirring. The attitude of France, Spain, Germany, even England, towards the Papacy was only partly the result of a revulsion in feeling against the abuses and weaknesses of the Catholic Church. Far more important was the stimulus which came from the quickening of a new spirit galvanizing these nation states to life. Nationalist aspirations were beginning to disintegrate the Europe of the Middle Ages. Geographical expressions were becoming self-conscious states craving after independence, monarchy, self-centred political life. The new kingdoms were rapidly acquiring a sense of their own power and importance. Under masterful monarchs they were growing tenacious of their rights. The more advanced among them were becoming aggressive. Europe was seething with diplomatic rivalries and national aspirations. The future lay with these young states. Their challenge to the old world of Empire and Papacy was decisive, and if we would appreciate the new era into which England was being carried after 1485, we must make the acquaintance of the nation states which were taking the lead and shaping the problems of Europe.

No state had been more fortunate than France, none was so prepared to take the lead. The second half of the fifteenth century had been one of uninterrupted growth, and with Louis XI. (1461–83) came the end of the Middle Ages so far as that country was concerned. With cunning statecraft he achieved the consolidation of French resources, and on all frontiers additions of territory had been made. Nor was that all. Growth was accompanied by much internal consolidation. By financial reforms, the removal of the more dangerous of feudal abuses, the encouragement of industry and trade, and the determined assertion of the royal power, Louis XI. left France a strong, consolidated nation state. Under his successors, Charles VIII. (1483–98) and Louis XII. (1498–1515), French nationalism became aggressive. Before the eyes of Charles VIII. there hovered dreams of empire. He saw himself taking Constantinople, driving the Turk out of Europe, winning for himself an imperial crown. The way to realization seemed to him to lie in Italy, and thus was born that wild venture of the Italian wars which marked the beginning of modern times and set the problems for sixteenth-century history.

Italy was an attractive prey for such designs. Its city states, rich, jealous of each other, hating and fearing the Papacy, which played for power and territory in Italy by controlling a balance amongst them, were fertile fields for political schemers to sow. Intent on their own rivalries, unable as a result to unite into a nation, they were ready to seek help in their internecine strife wherever help was forthcoming. Thus France and Spain found their way into Italian politics, and the feuds of the city states controlled the currents of European diplomacy.

For Spain at the end of the fifteenth century the future hardly appeared as bright as it did for

France, but a beginning had been made. Obstacles to national unity were great. Christianity struggling with Mohammedanism in southern Spain, and the separatist impulses of Aragon, Castile, and Portugal were problems not easy to solve. By the marriage (1469) of Ferdinand of Aragon (1479–1516) and Isabella of Castile (1474–1504) the way was opened up for unity, but it could not be achieved all at once. Only a very shrewd judge could have seen that the two rulers would succeed in driving the Moors out of Spain, establish strong government, and begin a movement towards expansion which would end in bringing Spain to the place of first importance in Europe. The ultimate chances of Spanish success in the sixteenth century were assured, but when Henry VII. came to the throne the signs of it were hardly visible.

In such a world and amongst such problems Henry Tudor was called upon to play his part. How small a part it was will best be realized by remembering the nature of these problems and the insignificance of England when it is compared with the other European powers with which it had to deal. What had England, or Henry, to do with the difficulties troubling continental statesmen ? At first sight it would appear that in the maze of European politics the English king could have no part. The questions at issue did not affect his country, the weakness of his own position seemed to render him a nonentity. In the early years of his reign his difficulties at home made it essential for him to concentrate his attention upon English politics, and the consequences of fifteenth-century history seemed to make insularity inevitable. With a depleted treasury and no credit he had none of the requisites for a spirited foreign policy. He had won a crown, but before he was likely to win the approval of Europe it would have to be proved that he was able to keep it. To attempt to force himself into foreign politics would be suicidal unless he could be certain of success, and the disadvantages of his position seemed to render the chances of such success extremely remote.

Despite such apparently overwhelming arguments, however, there were some weighty considerations which made a policy of insular inactivity impossible for him. They were not all in evidence constantly throughout the reign, for naturally their influence fluctuated with changing conditions, but, taken together, they comprise the forces dictating Henry's foreign policy. If each of them is examined, it will be possible to see the direction in which they forced him to move. To gain such a general impression is much more useful than it would be to make a mere chronological survey of the leading events in the diplomatic history of the period, for what is lost in chronological sequence will be more than regained if a clear idea of the motives actuating Henry in his foreign policy can be acquired. The chief of these influences may be easily summarized. First in time, if not in importance, were the complications arising from the obligations contracted by Henry in the days of his exile. These led to important results in the

early years of the reign. More permanent influences were those consequent on his succession to
the throne. The desire to consolidate his position
and the need to crush rebellion reacted upon
foreign policy, while ambition to found a dynasty,
and strengthen it by marriage alliances with
powers whose assistance would be worth having,
is the constant *motif* running through Henry's
schemes. Finally, when he had achieved success,
his designs for the prosperity of his country led
to the attempt to make commercial alliances. A
rough chronological division may be used to
emphasize the phases when the varying motives
were important. From 1485 until 1501 Henry
was mainly influenced by previous obligations, the
need for security, and the search for a marriage
alliance. After 1501 commercial interests loomed
larger, but the breakdown of his earlier marriage
negotiations reacted on his policy and led to the
less important and less satisfactory attempts at
further marriage alliances.

The obligations which Henry had incurred
before he came to the throne were felt immediately
after he began to reign. They led to action very
different from what might have been predicted
of a king whose interests should have made him
seek peace. Gratitude bound him to two powers
—France and Brittany. From Anne of Beaujeu,
regent for Charles VIII. of France, Henry had
received assistance for the expedition which ended
at Bosworth, for Richard's ventures in foreign
affairs had not been in the interests of France.
From Duke Francis II. of Brittany Henry had

received many kindnesses and hospitality. Neither obligation was forgotten. Unfortunately, they were incompatible. French statesmen, following out the policy of territorial extension mapped for them by Louis XI., aimed at the annexation of Brittany, and although Henry, in 1485 and 1486, gave evidence of his desire to keep at peace with France, his own interests, coupled with the French menace to the security of Brittany, pushed him towards war. With the death of the Duke of Brittany in September 1488, and the resultant French claim to wardship over the young duchess, the position became more intolerable. Upon Henry devolved the duty of coming to her protection. Perhaps the chivalrous though wild-headed expedition of Woodville in May 1488 was not undertaken quite so much against Henry's wishes as he tried to make the world believe ; but whether it was or not, it made war inevitable. In 1489, and again in 1491, he was drawn deeper into conflict with France. The complicated diplomatic activity of those years was brought to nothing by the woman in the case. In December 1491 Anne, Duchess of Brittany, married Charles VIII. France thus gained all she had been seeking. It was not easy, however, for Henry to climb out of his difficulties without justifying his policy by war. In October 1492 he crossed to France. His heart was not in the war, and his main object was to use this gesture in order to make a peace. In November 1492 he succeeded. By the peace of Etaples England and France settled their difficulties. The usual agreements to live in amity and establish a *status quo ante* in commercial matters was overshadowed by the favourable financial terms England obtained. The king of France agreed to pay the English king a sum of 745,000 gold crowns in instalments, and Henry thankfully recalled his troops from an expedition which had demonstrated the possibility of turning warfare into a paying business proposition. Thus ended the adventures which had come to Henry as a result of his obligations. Meanwhile the negotiations had given him an opportunity to deal with some of the other considerations governing his policy in those early years.

The experiences of the period 1485–92 had served to show Henry the weaknesses of his own position, and the value of diplomacy as a means of overcoming them. Much was at stake which was of greater importance than the fate of Brittany, and Henry's aims were wider than they appear if the Breton question is regarded as the sole objective of his policy during those early years. Throughout that period Henry's first consideration was the security of his own position in England, and he was quick to see that foreign policy could be made to serve that end. The advantages to be gained from an alliance with a foreign power were real. The prestige following on such an understanding, however small the power with whom it was made, was bound to be an advantage, since it meant the recognition of Henry's title in the eyes of the world. Not only would an alliance bring prestige abroad, but it was in itself a powerful argument in his favour at

home. For the king who succeeded in gaining
support abroad was obviously impressing contemporaries with the safety of his position and his
superiority over rivals to the throne. A foreign
alliance, then, would be proof to Englishmen that
Henry had come to stay. More important, however, were the direct results accruing to Henry in
his dealings with the rebellions which he had to
withstand. It has already been suggested that
the great theme of his reign during the period
1485–1501 was the king's struggle with usurpers.
His difficulties were complicated because such
plots were not, on the whole, demonstrations of
anti-Tudor feeling on the part of Englishmen, but
were rather adventures stimulated by enemies
abroad. A small party within the country was
the tool of foreigners eager to destroy Henry and
his house. The evil spirit of such ventures was
Margaret of Burgundy, sister of Edward IV.,
prompted in all her enthusiasms by the uncompromising fury of a dynastic feud, and ready
to assist any adventurers, willing to believe any
story, if it could be turned to account in the
perpetuation of an undying hostility to the Tudor
cause. Behind each of the risings of the reign the
machinations of foreign schemers can be traced.
The adventures of a Lambert Simnel or a Perkin
Warbeck were for the most part worked out on
English soil, but behind the plots were the shady
adventurers of foreign courts, while the resources
of the rebels would have been considerably smaller
had they been deprived of what came to them
from abroad. In the face of such conditions it

was essential for Henry to look abroad. Strong
government and active measures in England would
go far to scotch rebellion, but there could be no
guarantee of safety until Henry had protected
himself by approaches to foreign countries so as
to make some of them, at any rate, unsafe hiding-
places for the rebels who fled from England.

How could such friendships be cultivated?
There could be only one solution, and that was
the skilful manipulation of marriage alliances
within the royal house. It was the approved
sixteenth-century material for diplomatic activity.
More than any one else in Europe, Henry VII.
had to make careful use of his children in order
to obtain the best results for himself and his
country. Arthur, the son born in September
1486, symbolized the union of the roses. Unless
his marriage was carefully arranged it might well
become the symbol of disunion. To marry him
in England to a Lancastrian or a Yorkist would be
to reopen a newly-healed wound. To avoid such
an error by a foreign alliance became the object
of Henry's statecraft, and his objective was soon
found to be Spain.

It is doubtful whether Henry realized the full
significance of the choice. When, in 1488, his
attention was turned towards Spain, the prospects
for that country were not very propitious, and
Henry's choice was more largely the result of
circumstance than of any great prescience on his
part. The complications of the Breton question
made it impossible for Henry to stand on his own
against France, and the search for a supporter

naturally led him to Spain, where the Breton issue was being watched with considerable interest. Spain, like other European countries, had begun the policy of consolidation of territory by the marriage of Ferdinand and Isabella. The next step was to secure the provinces of Roussillon and Cerdagne from France, and the Breton question offered a favourable opportunity for intervention. It was in these circumstances that Henry VII. began, in March 1488, to negotiate with the Spanish monarchs. Neither party was easily satisfied, and it was not until March 1489 that the treaty of Medina del Campo was drawn up. That agreement was to be the key to Anglo-Spanish relations for a very considerable time, and its clauses will repay a little study. They reveal quite clearly that Henry was the weaker party in the bargaining, and that Spain's comparative indifference enabled her to secure the better terms. On the question of the marriage alliance which was so near to Henry's heart, he was successful, for it was to be concluded when the children reached marriageable age. Even on this matter, however, Spanish interests were very carefully safeguarded. The young princess's dowry was to be 200,000 scudos, reckoning each scudo at 4s. 2d. One half was to be paid when she arrived in England, and the remainder within the next two years. She was to receive the third part of the revenues of Wales, Cornwall, and Chester, which was to be guaranteed at not less than 23,000 or 25,000 crowns, but this sum was to be increased if she became queen. The Spanish sovereigns, for their part, promised to send the princess to England suitably apparelled and provided with jewels becoming to her rank. On the political side the treaty engaged both parties to a true friendship, reciprocal commercial privileges, and a pledge not to harbour each other's rebels. But Spain had the better of the bargain. If the king of France voluntarily restored Normandy and Aquitaine to England, Henry might conclude peace with him whether Spain agreed or not. If, on the other hand, the king of France restored Roussillon and Cerdagne to Spain, the latter might make peace with or without England's consent. Henry's readiness to agree to such an arrangement is the most eloquent comment on his anxiety for the Spanish marriage. The cession of the provinces of Roussillon and Cerdagne to Spain was so small a matter that it might well be regarded as a distinct possibility. But to get France to give up Normandy and Aquitaine voluntarily was as feasible as to ask her to undo all the history her sons had made since the Hundred Years' War. The truth of the matter was, of course, that Spain was hoping to use England in the working out of her own plans.

In such circumstances began that contact between England and Spain which was to be fraught with such momentous consequences. They could as yet hardly be foreseen, for the full development of Spanish power had not really begun, nor indeed had the tangled implications of the Spanish marriage policy been evolved. The marriage itself did not take place immediately. Spain played on the clause postponing the marriage until the children were of age, and was unwilling to trust the princess to Henry's care before they were quite certain that the English king had made good his position in England. The haggling over satisfactory terms was to continue for many years, and the diplomatic papers of the period reflect the shameless mercenary spirit in which the monarchs of England and Spain approached these negotiations. To describe the sequel would be to extend this account beyond all bounds. It must be sufficient to say that it was not until November 15, 1501, that the discussion finally ended in the marriage of Catherine and Arthur, amidst the enthusiastic cheers of the crowds gathered to witness the elaborate ceremony at St. Paul's in London.

The marriage is a landmark in the foreign policy of Henry VII., for it was the culmination of years of patient diplomatic negotiations, and the outward manifestation that he was considered to be sufficiently master of England to be looked upon as an ally of Spain. A rapid series of events was to show how frail are the foundations on which human hopes are sometimes built, and what had become accomplished fact was soon as though it had not been. By April 2, 1502, the young Spanish princess was a widow. All the work of years had been done in vain. In less than a year afterwards Henry himself was a widower. His queen died on February 4, 1503. From 1502–9 the old narrative of searching for marriage alliances occupies a great part of the history of the reign.

This time it was Spain's turn to be anxious. Henry was none too scrupulous a diplomatist, and while Catherine remained in England he was naturally in a strong position. As soon as the news of the death of Prince Arthur reached Spain, Ferdinand and Isabella issued instructions to their ambassador to reclaim from the king of England the 100,000 scudos paid as the first instalment of the princess's marriage portion, to demand her dowry, and to beg Henry to send Catherine back to Spain as soon as possible. But they were still hoping for the best, for at the same time they gave the ambassador authority to arrange with Henry a marriage between their daughter and his second son, Henry, the new Prince of Wales. The wheel had gone full circle. Henry's policy of consolidation had justified itself. His alliance was worth having, and Henry could afford to assume a most independent attitude in the knowledge that Spain was not in a position to quibble about terms. Not until June 23, 1503, was an agreement concluded, and even then the lapse of time consequent upon the necessary applications for a papal dispensation—since the marriage was within the prohibited degrees—eventually meant a delay which Henry was not anxious to avoid. As a result the marriage of Catherine and Henry did not take place until after Henry VII. was dead.

Important as the first Spanish marriage had been, these second negotiations were infinitely more important. They set the stage for a bigger drama than Henry or any one else amongst his contemporaries could have dreamed. But it was not these possibilities that caused the Spanish monarchs anxiety at the time. They were more seriously concerned at the frights Henry was deliberately manufacturing for them. In 1503 it was believed that he was thinking of marrying Catherine himself, and Spanish ingenuity was taxed to provide substitutes to prevent such a disaster. The last six years of his reign were largely taken up with such schemes, and the story is neither edifying nor important in the general narrative of English foreign policy. The suggestion of the Spanish monarchs as an alternative to the rumoured offer to Catherine was that Henry should marry their niece, Joanna of Naples. Henry considered the matter, and the instructions given to the ambassadors he sent to interview the lady is the most curious diplomatic document of the period. They were to be beauty specialists as well as ambassadors. Other schemes were also suggested. Henry toyed with the idea of a marriage with Margaret of Savoy, but that lady had other views on the subject. Another more repulsive idea was a marriage with Joanna, Queen of Castile, the death of whose husband, in 1506, had impaired her intellect. The comment of the Spanish ambassador was a cynical revelation of the diplomacy of the times. The marriage would not prevent hopes of a family, and he thought that was all England would care about. None of these schemes came to anything. They were interrupted by Henry's death.

Enough has been said to show that Henry was no mean exponent of the sixteenth-century art of arranging marriage alliances, and much more will have to be said later of the consequences directly issuing from his work. The motives dominating his diplomacy were not all, however, due to considerations of family alliance. As soon as he felt himself strong enough to hold his own, Henry aimed at schemes for the commercial advancement of his country, and no account of the factors shaping his foreign policy would give a true view of what he achieved if it failed to make a passing reference to his commercial negotiations.

The relations with Spain were not contracted without some recognition of the advantages of freedom for commercial development, although such arrangements were by no means Henry's sole contribution to the solution of this problem. From the beginning of the reign the significance of an extension of commercial enterprise was not lost on the king. He aimed at the stimulus of the wool trade and of the manufacture of cloth, and even in the midst of political complications he encouraged schemes for the development of English trade. There was reason for immediate action. Part of the legacy of the wars of the roses was a marked diminution in the extent of English commerce. Under cover of the disturbances in this country the Hansa merchants had driven the English out of their markets in the north of Europe, and Henry's early years saw negotiations to win back trading privileges in Denmark and other parts of the continent. Commercial policy was used as a handmaid to foreign politics. The English wool trade with the Low Countries had

49

long been a fruitful source of trade, and the demand for English wool gave Henry a diplomatic weapon he was not slow to use. In 1493 he showed how dangerous it could be to harbour English rebels, by forbidding all trade between England and Flanders. The effects of that ultimatum upon the cloth trade in the Low Countries soon showed how dangerous was the power in England's hands. Even more striking were the diplomatic victories by which Henry won advantages for English merchants. The most famous example was the trading agreement with Flanders in 1496. The title which was later given to it, the Intercursus Magnus, is indicative of the benefits it conferred upon English commerce. Its main importance lay in the settlement of free commercial intercourse between Burgundy and England. The tariff of dues payable by English and Flemish merchants was to be fixed at a rate not exceeding that which had been in force during the preceding fifty years. Fisheries were declared free, and in order to stimulate traffic between the two countries definite efforts were to be made to destroy the prevailing piracy which was such a menace to peaceful intercourse. The success of the treaty encouraged Henry, and when the opportunity arose he endeavoured to screw greater advantages for his subjects. About 1504 fresh political difficulties were making trade impossible, when Henry had the good fortune to get the Archduke Philip more or less under his control by the shipwreck of that prince on the English coast. A treaty was signed in 1506 whose later title—the

Intercursus Malus—suggests its unfairness. By this agreement the rates fixed in 1496 were to remain in force, but English merchants were to receive further advantages by being exempted from local tolls in the Low Countries. In addition they were to be given the right of carrying on retail trade in all parts of the Netherlands except Flanders. The treaty was not such a success as is sometimes suggested. It was obviously unfair, and when Philip died in 1506 the matter was reopened. As a result, a treaty was signed in 1507 which remedied some of the disadvantages. A return was made to the clauses of the Intercursus Magnus, and the grant of rights of retail trade was annulled. With this more equitable arrangement relations between the two countries continued until Henry's death.

Closely connected with commercial policy is another question deserving of notice. It is introduced because it suggests an important factor in European history rather than because it reflects credit on Henry VII. It would be wrong to use the meagre evidence of Henry's interest in exploration work as material for constructing a eulogy of him as a far-sighted pioneer of English expansion. That he did something to assist explorers is true, but it was not much, nor was it the result of any systematic policy he had developed. His proffered assistance to Columbus was made too late, and in 1493 Henry knew that the benefit of that discoverer's work had been reaped by his own rival, the king of Spain. He gave some later indications of interest in this work by helping

Cabot in 1496, and although the condition of that explorer's licence stated he was going out at his own expense, it is believed that Henry helped him with a ship. In 1501 he made grants to three Portuguese merchants setting out on a voyage of discovery. When all is said, however, Henry's interest was not great, and the merit for the little exploration that went on during his reign must be laid to the credit of Bristol merchants. To say this is not to condemn Henry, since he could hardly be expected to risk his scanty resources upon unpromising enterprises, any more than he could be expected to look into the future and see how great the advantages of this work were to be for Spain. Yet, the inactivity of England in the age of discovery should be read as another illustration of how unimportant the country really was, and Henry may be spared some credit for the little he did in helping work which was not to be a characteristic feature of English seamanship until the period with which we are concerned in this book had drawn to its close.

Such were some of the considerations shaping the actions of Henry VII. in his dealings with his contemporaries. They will be sufficient to indicate the interaction between English and continental politics, which made participation in foreign affairs essential. The cross currents they set in motion could only be estimated by a more detailed study of policy than is possible in the limits at our disposal. The main question that calls for an answer here is that which seeks the general criticism that is to be passed upon Henry's work abroad. As a policy it was not heroic, but it was reliable. It was above all things a policy of peace. Once freed from the entanglements with France, Henry concentrated upon remaining at peace with the world, and in the wider issues of European politics he played no part. True he took sides in the continental rivalry by joining the Holy League in 1496, but he had no intention of taking an active part, nor could any Pope succeed in persuading him to abandon his insular position in order to chase Turks out of Europe. It is easy to be wise after the event by criticizing him for his alliance with Spain, but he can be justified. He was—as a contemporary said he always liked to be—on the winning side, and the developments of later times directly resultant upon the Spanish marriage were not such as he could be expected to predict. In his own day the link with Spain was a spectacular vindication of his strength, and by it England took the first step towards a higher position in the eyes of European contemporaries. Henry gave his country peace and prestige. There were no two things she needed more acutely at the opening of the period, and what she would be capable of doing when she had obtained them the immediate future was to show.

CHAPTER IV

CHURCH AND STATE

THERE are many problems to be solved by those who seek the meaning of the English Reformation movement, but two impressions it leaves stand out so clearly that they may be accepted as the starting-point of any study. The first is that the Reformation was pre-eminently a problem of practical politics, absorbing the attention not merely of English statesmen but of every seriously minded English subject as a living issue in the political life of the times. The second is quite as definite. The Reformation was a religious movement concerned with deep spiritual realities, opening issues which revealed the springs of human life, and dealing with mysteries beyond the borderland where life meets death. Now the whole problem of the English Reformation centres round the interaction of these two truths. The ultimate question to be asked will be found here. How came it that the mysteries of religious experience and the spiritual aspirations of man could be turned into a question of practical politics? Why were the arguments of theologians the inspiration for acts of parliament, and the

54

deeds of politicians the factors deciding the fate
of the Church ?

The modern world, by its relegation of religious
experience to a remote corner of life, finds it hard
to answer such questions, or even to visualize the
situation which they reflect. Only by conscious
effort can it reach the standpoint of the Tudor
mind, but if we are to seek with any hope of
success for the inner meaning of the Reformation
that conscious effort must be made. The point
of view can be described more easily than it can
be attained. For if we wish to understand the
attitude of Tudor men towards the religio-political
problems of their day, we must first of all realize
how great a part the Church, before the Reformation, played in every sphere of their lives. This
is not easy. That Church eludes us, for we have
to look for it across the fields of time, and the
mists of religious controversy hang low upon the
landscape. For some the Reformation is a catas-
trophe that overwhelmed the Church in England and crushed the most important institution
of the age. To them that vanished institution
stands beyond the reach of criticism, and they are
suspicious of any talk of faults. For others, however, the Reformation is a constructive movement,
and their attitude towards events is very different.
They reserve their eulogies for what that movement did, and the Church of its creation seems to
them a splendid contrast to what had gone before.
Neither attitude will satisfy the historian. Before
he can understand the Reformation he must view
again, with eyes unclouded by religious partisan-

ship, the Church as it flourished in England before the breach with Rome. If the institution he finds is less impressive than its partisans believe, it is also more to be lamented than its enemies assert, and in the cold light of criticism it suggests more adequately than the rhetoric of partisans can do the real reasons why it underwent a revolutionary change.

The approach must be gradual. The first thing to realize about the Church in England in the fifteenth century is that it was the symbol of a great ideal, and the second that it was the handiwork of man. That the ideal was not always even approached, much less attained, will not arouse wonder, but emphasis upon its human limitations will engender a spirit of tolerance in the study of the institution, and will make the transition from the Church in England to the Church of England a process more intelligible than that suggested by the idea of catastrophic change. The following pages are written to suggest some of the ideals in the minds of the best men of the fifteenth century, and to indicate the potential value of these ideals for the world. When that has been done it will be easier to show how and why some of them were growing a little dim, and where the fabric of an age-old institution was crumbling into dust.

The results of a search for signs of popular hostility to the Church in the later Middle Ages must not blind us to the true state of things. Here and there it is easy to find evidence of the unpopularity of ecclesiastical men and the things they represent, hostility due to factors that will not long remain hidden from us ; but on the whole the impression to be gathered is that there was a widespread devotion to the institution which played so large a part in human life. Nor is it hard to explain such devotion. It was due to the ideals the Church represented.

A modern critic of the later Middle Ages has said that " no other epoch has laid so much stress as the expiring Middle Ages on the thought of death. An everlasting call of *memento mori* resounds through life." The thought has some bearing on Church history. It was the claim of the Church that it held the keys to everlasting life, and its supremacy originated in its right to be the interpreter of the laws of a kingdom not of this world. It was as the guide and protector of the souls of men that the Church had a place in this world, and the implications of those responsibilities explain the secret of its worldly power. The thought of its ministers guiding the pilgrim to heaven seized hold of the imagination of men, and their functions as curators of souls gave them their power on earth. Popular thought could not afford the risk of flippant scepticism. When all was said and done, at last came Death. An institution able to help in that hour of need was not to be repulsed. Masses for the souls of the dead, bequests in wills for works of charity, religious benefactions—all these were pious duties not to be neglected by any one who could afford them. They were the manifestations of the world's faith in the Church. There might be careless living, irreverent comment, even open criticism of the Church upon earth, but the ultimate fact was never far from mind. Before the judgment seat only the Church could intercede. An institution with such a prerogative did not find it hard to enforce obedience.

It was this final scene which dominated the relations of the Church with mankind. Cure of souls implied more than support in the hour of death. It meant control during the whole of the earthly pilgrimage, and the ever-present Church had its tasks to perform at all points in a man's life. There was a ritual in daily life, a ritual only the Church could create. From birth to death men lived underneath the shadow of the Church, and the solemn ceremonies which were the landmarks on their way were ceremonies organized by the Church. Christenings, marriages, burials—these were rites that entered into the existence of even the most ordinary of mortals, and they called for the ministrations of the Church. Such personal relationship left a deep impression, and its influence was strengthened by the more resplendent —if less intimate—ceremonials which the Church had evolved. To speak of the dramatic beauty of the Mass, the splendours of festivals, the aural and ocular recreation provided in sermons, pictures, architecture, would be to write half the history of the Middle Ages, while a survey which omits the influence of the confessional ignores a factor whose benefits and disadvantages were alike almost incalculable. It must be enough to suggest that such influences loomed large in the lives of the men of the time. They gave to the Church a control over human thought not easily estimated, and a power of attracting the reverence and—in the majority of cases—the love of men.

The safety of the soul involved more than ceremonies upon the road of life. The men to whom human government was entrusted needed advisers. The Church, attracting to itself in the way it did the cream of intellect and education, could supply that need, and in the counsels of earthly rulers the hierarchy of the clergy had an honoured place. Nor was the Church without its share in the smaller affairs of more ordinary mortals. It added to its functions of spiritual consoler, teacher, guide, the no less important work of the judge. If the soul were to be preserved it must be controlled and chastened, and none could do that save only the minister of the Church. Thus there crept into the lives of ordinary individuals a spiritual power affecting them at every step on their way. It was a power that was in the main exercised on their behalf, and it won from them reverence and love. There were, however, occasions when it was less easy to appreciate the motives at work, and then there were indications of emotions of another kind. They were to increase with the passing of the years.

How far-reaching the activities of the Church were in these spheres can best be gleaned by a study of ecclesiastical jurisdiction. For the good of souls it was essential that those who dared to question the teaching of the Church should be checked. According to canon law heresy was punishable by burning, and the growth of heretical opinions in the fifteenth century led to statutes in 1401 and 1414, which enforced the powers of the bishops in these cases by giving them the assistance of the civil power. Nor was heresy the only offence with which ecclesiastical courts concerned themselves. Neglect of Church services, perjury, witchcraft, and breaches of morality ranging from immorality to drunkenness, were all matters which brought offenders into the hands of the ecclesiastical judge. Such sins could easily be avoided by the good Christian, but that did not mean that he thereby withdrew from ecclesiastical control. For the ideal of the Church as the abiding influence in a man's life gave it other duties. All the things to which the marriage ceremony was linked fell within its jurisdiction. The validity of the ceremony itself, the capacity to marry, the lawfulness of the ceremony, and the legitimacy of the children, were grave questions which might at any moment affect not merely a man's eternal destiny, but also his material position in this world. Questions of inheritance to property, for instance, were seriously affected by the answers that the Church gave to questions concerning legitimacy such as those suggested above. So, too, the complications arising from death fell within the competence of the Church. Wills, the granting of probate, the supervision of the disposal of the goods of the deceased person—these, and innumerable issues arising out of them, brought most people into direct contact with the Church at important crises in their lives.

Such, then, were some of the more important

implications of the idea of cure of souls as it
affected the relationship of the Church to the
world. They will suggest the tremendous significance of the institution to the men of the time,
for no contact could be so impressive as that which
brought the worldly affairs of mankind within the
grasp of the Church. But this material aspect
must not be stressed without a passing reference
to another feature of religious life. From what
has been said it will be clear that the ideal of the
Church was to help men to live in this world.
It had another work to do. It sought to enable
some of them to live out of the world. Monasticism, in theory and practice, is a suggestive topic,
but it is not one to be taken up at this point.
Here it must be sufficient to indicate that the
monastic ideal was an essential feature of the
period, and that an organization enabling men—
and women—to live apart from the world in com-
munities planned to make possible an exposition
of the true religious life, formed an integral part
of the Church catholic. Like other religious
ideals of the period, we shall find monasticism
less attractive in the practice than in the theory of
the age, and the results of the failure to realize the
ideal will play no small part in the later history
of the period with which we are concerned.

It would be wrong to take this sketch as an
adequate description of what the Church meant
to the men of the time. Criticism of an institution
is easier than the recognition of its merits. But
these points of contact between Church and State
are important, and so with all its limitations this

sketch had to be made in order to suggest two important truths on which Reformation history rests. In the first place, it proves that the organized Church of the later Middle Ages put forward claims to a large share in the life of every individual. In the second place, there can be little question that those claims were freely admitted for the most part by the men of the time. It is only when these two ideas are grasped that the real puzzle of the Reformation presents itself, and it is only then, too, that the answer to the puzzle can be even faintly seen. It will be clear before we have gone very far that the ideals represented in the claims the Church made were only partially achieved. But that did not destroy all its influence, for there were within the institution many who strove after these ideals, and their unfailing efforts in well-doing won for them and their Church the support and, in many cases, the genuine love of the generation they sought to serve.

The very nature of the claims to which churchmen in their most exalted moments aspired involved factors with a questionable influence which worked directly towards the undermining of loyal devotion. Fear of the unknown, the awful mystery of death, struck terror into the hearts of men, and acted as a bond which drew them near the Church. No trickery was needed to keep them there. Superstitious ideas grew of their own accord, needing little encouragement from priests, and in the mouths of enthusiasts the horrors of a future state, or the advantages of an anthropomorphic heaven, were almost unconsciously

used to inspire emotions the reverse of Christian.
It is easier to arouse sensations than to quicken
thought. Superstitious beliefs and practices are
more easily inculcated than true religion. Fear
was too often the substitute for love, denunciatory
preaching took the place of teaching, and the
religious beliefs of the masses were a blending of
pious sentiments and absurd superstitions whose
influence could not be other than bad. Image
worship, invocation of saints, the observance of
religious forms from which all meaning had long
since fled, these took the place of intelligent belief
in the fundamental truths for which the Church
stood. The shrines of saints and the tombs of
martyrs were the objectives of pilgrimages, and the
religion of many was little more than the mass of
superstition gleaned at such places. Erasmus
was no friend of such things, but in his description
of the shrine of Our Lady at Walsingham, in
Norfolk, which he gave in his *Colloquies*, he was
evidently describing what he had seen, and the
picture of superstition he paints is near the truth.
Again, when he visited the tomb of St. Thomas
of Canterbury, he saw " the point of the sword
with which the top of the head of the good prelate
was wounded, and some of his brains that were
beaten out, to make sure work on't. We most
religiously kissed the sacred rust of this weapon,
out of love to the Martyr. Leaving this place,
we went down into a vault under ground : to that
there belong two shewers of relicks. The first
thing they shew you is the skull of the Martyr as
it was bored through ; the upper part is left open

to be kiss'd, all the rest is covered over with silver."
The box in which the other bones of the saint
rested was of gold. "Everything sparkled and
shined with very large and scarce Jewels, some of
them bigger than a goose's egg." This is a scoffer's
pen at work, but a Venetian visitor to England
about 1500 bears out the truth of Erasmus's words.
The magnificence of the tomb surpassed his belief.
"Notwithstanding its great size [it] is entirely
covered over with plates of gold; but the gold is
scarcely visible from the variety of precious stones
with which it is studded, such as sapphires,
diamonds, rubies, balas rubies and emeralds;
and on every side that the eye turns something
more beautiful than the other appears. And these
beauties of nature are enhanced by human skill,
for the gold is carved and engraved in beautiful
designs both large and small, and agates, jaspers,
and cornelians set in relievo, some of the cameos
being of such a size that I do not dare to mention
it; but everything is left far behind by a ruby,
not larger than a man's thumbnail, which is set
to the right of the altar. The church is rather
dark, and particularly so where the shrine is
placed, and when we went in to see it the sun was
nearly gone down, and the weather was cloudy:
yet I saw that ruby as well as if I had it in my
hand." The day was to dawn when that ruby
would be set in a ring—upon the finger of Henry
VIII. !

Such wealth, accumulated largely through
appeals to superstition, is symbolical of the way
in which the Church had been the ideal of former

times. Property had accumulated around all
churches, abbeys, monasteries. Its distribution
among the poor and needy was rarer than it should
have been. It brought complications, since ecclesiastical estates had to be managed, and the churchmen whose duty it was to administer them became
above all else men of business. A secular spirit
crept into the Church. Nor were the affairs of
state to which churchmen were called away as
advisers any less dangerous. Bishops were busied
over many things, but they were chiefly the things
of this world. They lived the lives of statesmen
and ambassadors, but their worldliness was poor
example for the laity. It is not surprising if there
were occasions when the hungry sheep looked
up and were not fed. Nor were all the opportunities offered to the Church taken up by the
higher order of ecclesiastics. Monks, friars,
parish priests, were engrossed with their own
affairs, and many opportunities to do good in the
world were lost through the self-seeking of the
clergy.

That the life of the Church was stained by vices
which ought not to be associated with it is a fact
that only prejudice of the deepest kind would try
to deny. The problem is not one to be passed
over lightly, but it is difficult to decide to what
extent the evils were common. While it is undoubtedly true that murder, immorality, crimes
of a more or less heinous nature, were committed
by parish clergy, and that there are numerous
examples of monasteries where disorderly living
was notorious, at the same time it would be absurd

65

to condemn the Church as an institution for the faults of members to whom rules of celibacy and rigid discipline were unattainable ideals. So much has been written in recent years to absolve the Church, that to-day there is a danger of going to the other extreme. Let it be said at once that much of the alleged evidence formerly employed to prove the complete breakdown of ecclesiastical morality is now known to be unsafe testimony, and that exceptional cases must not be used for historical generalizations. Even so, when due allowance for these facts has been made, it is still impossible to ignore completely the responsibility of the Church. Perhaps the nearest approach to truth that it is possible to attain is the thought that what really matters is not the number of evil-doers to be found amongst the clergy. The really impressive fact is that evil existed in sufficient quantity to make it possible for the satirists of the age to pour scorn on the Church by doing little more than repeating accusations that were well known to their readers. The tirades of a Starkey or a Simon Fish may be violent exaggerations. That they should be put forward with every hope that they would be believed is a damning proof that there were ugly features in Church life. And they were features that men who were by no means hostile to organized Christianity found it hard to ignore.

The theme of the ubiquity of Church influence must lead sooner or later to a problem as old as government. Where was the line of demarcation to be drawn between the affairs of the State and

those of the Church. What belonged to Cæsar
and what to God ? From one point of view that
is the fundamental problem in the English Reformation, and the way in which the issue was gradually developed is one of the most clearly defined
features of ecclesiastical history under Henry VII.
On the one hand was a king avowedly working
to suppress the feudal privileges inimical to his
royal authority. On the other hand was a great
institution whose vaguely defined privileges
dragged it inevitably into conflict with him. For
if the Church were efficient, achieving its ideal of
sharing in the affairs of all men, then it was bound
to go on increasing its power and sphere of influence, with the result that it was inevitably fated
to come into opposition with the king. If, on the
other hand, it were inefficient, then it would abuse
the privileges it possessed, and be an obstacle to
the royal plans. In either case, the conflict between king and Church was hardly to be avoided.
Signs of its approach could be seen under Henry
VII., though the cloud that presaged it was little
bigger than a man's hand.

Henry VII. was far too much a man of his age
and too cautious to develop revolutionary ideas
of his relationship to the Pope. Loyal son of the
Church as he was, he established cordial relations
with Rome as soon as he gained his throne. The
Pope recognized his accession in a generous bull.
Those friendly relations were maintained throughout the reign. Henry thought it worth while to
interest the Pope in his cause when rebels were
a source of trouble, and the spirit of the following

letter will convey more eloquently than much comment could do the nature of Henry's attitude to the Vicar of Christ. In 1487 a criminal had spoken contemptuously of Christ and the Pope. " Wherefore," says Henry, " he instantly fell dead upon the ground, and his face and body immediately became blacker than soot itself, and shortly afterwards the corpse emitted such a stench that no one soever could approach it. Verily we give thanks to Almighty God, who of His ineffable mercy has exhibited in our kingdom so great a miracle concerning the Christian faith." Such orthodoxy well deserved the gift of the papal sword and cap of maintenance which Henry received upon three occasions from three Popes—Innocent VIII., Alexander VI., and Julius II.

Below the surface there was sterner stuff. Symbolical is a letter from a papal agent telling his master how a money-box had been opened which Henry allowed the Church to have at court. " We found in it eleven pounds eleven shillings," he says, " which result made our hearts sink within us, for there were present the King, the Queen, the mother of the King, and the mother of the Queen, besides dukes, earls, and marquises and other lords and ambassadors, so that we expected to have had much more." Henry never gave more than he could help. His caution never allowed the Papacy to get the better of him, and in his letter refusing to be drawn into the crusade he shows skill in evading the difficult issue while still remaining a true son of the Church.

Tact solved many problems of the reign, but

the very nature of Henry's policy forced the issue
between him and the Church. When it came he
was uncompromising. Appointment of bishops
was kept closely in his hands. Papal patronage
was curtailed by his insistence on the appointment
of Englishmen, and the path for the future was
indicated by some permissions for visitations of
monasteries. There were deeper problems. Half
of Henry's reign was spent in stripping overmighty subjects of their liberties. It needed no
strong Erastian theories to bring the man with
such a policy in conflict with the Church. In the
early years of the reign churchmen had a hint
when the abbot of Westminster made great show
of his privileges in the law courts. He was told
that it was not wise for him to bring his franchises
into discussion. The reason was soon apparent.
Any Church privileges standing in the way of
sound administration of law were doomed. That
meant, in effect, an attack upon two things—
benefit of clergy, and the right of sanctuary.
Both were privileges jealously guarded by the
Church. Both had become serious hindrances to
sound administration of law. The former—originally a privilege of the clergy to be free from lay
jurisdiction—had been so extended that it had
come to mean that almost any one capable of
reading could avoid lay courts and be subjected
to a different standard of punishment in spiritual
courts. The latter—which meant that a criminal
who took refuge in a church could not be taken
out of it to prison, but had to be allowed to abjure
the country—had led to grave abuses, rendered

worse in the case of the larger sanctuaries, where men were allowed to remain as " sanctuary men." Here they had homes from which, on occasion, they went out into the world to break the law. While these privileges were in existence no sound rule of law could be enforced. Henry met the challenge by decreasing the number of those qualified to claim benefit of clergy, and by preparing the way for a considerable diminution of the privilege of sanctuary. It was not the end of these privileges, but it was an ominous prelude to the coming challenge of State to Church.

If the time were ever to come for an assault on the position, privileges, and wealth of the Church, the men to lead the attack would have to be ruthless. In its teachings lay the strength of the Church, and those who would dare to storm the temple would have to be deaf to the voice of its priests. Excommunication, interdict, anathema, were weapons of whose efficacy Church history provided ample proof, and those who would brave these things would need the staying power that could only be gained from independent minds and critical reasons fearless of superstitious threats. Such qualities were not to be gained in a moment, and Henry VII.'s reign saw only the beginnings of growth. Yet no survey of the Church of the late fifteenth century can afford to omit the signs of the times. Early in the reign there were indications that the spirit of criticism lived, and that the teachings of the clergy were not falling only on minds ready to accept all that was being offered them. To speak as though Lollardy was rampant in early Tudor times would be to over-estimate the strength of a movement which had been ruthlessly dealt with earlier in the century, but it would be ostrich-like to refuse to see that persecution had not completely wiped it out. Henry VII., good churchman as he was, argued with a heretic before he burned him, and his bishops occasionally heard language they could hardly have enjoyed. In 1489 the archbishop of Canterbury was hearing the recantation of one Stephen Swallow, who had uttered strange here-sies against the sacraments, called the Pope rude names, and denied the existence of purgatory. He thought the Church of Rome the synagogue of Satan, and denied that the Pope was the Vicar of Christ. One Swallow does not make a reforma-tion, but there were heretics about in sufficient numbers to form a nucleus for change. Men were talking, and when education had given them what they needed, they would have more to say. The future lay with education.

The many-sided renaissance movement had a deep significance in European history. It released the mediæval world from the bondage of scholastic learning, and brought again the spirit of classical culture into a world whose attention had been too closely centred upon the study of theology. Its abiding contribution to intellectual development, whatever the sphere in which it made itself felt, was that fresh spirit of curiosity which forced men to a new view of themselves, their fellows, and the world in which they lived. To attempt to trace the manifestations of such a spirit in all its developments would be a task which would extend this sketch far beyond the limits allotted to it, and would entail the inclusion of much that is not, strictly speaking, of importance in the story of English growth. But there are some features of the renaissance movement which had a direct bearing upon English history, and it is necessary to touch upon those special aspects of it which fit into the sequel of English development in early Tudor times.

Now the first thing always worth remembering when one deals with the intellectual development of England during this period is that the "new learning" was stirring in England in the reign of Henry VII. True, there had been some slight promise of such a movement in the fifteenth century, but for Henry's reign more than mere promise can be chronicled. The mediæval qualities of that monarch must not blind us to the signs of change, and the brilliant dawn of the reign of his successor should not be allowed to rob the reign of the first Tudor of what credit is due to it for the pioneer work done on behalf of intellectual growth. The renaissance movement owed its inspiration to the cultural influences that were reviving in Italy, and before there could be a renaissance elsewhere a contact had to be established with Italy. The lives of the English renaissance leaders show quite clearly that such relations were real in the time of the first Henry. Grocyn and Linacre were in Italy between 1485 and 1491. Colet returned to England after his wanderings there in 1496. By that time young Thomas More was an undergraduate who was already coming under the influence of the new thought through friendship with these men. To say that these students had come back from Italy is to say that they had begun to spread the new ideas they had imbibed, and from the middle of Henry VII.'s reign there was an active group of enthusiasts for the "new learning" at the universities. Their enthusiasm did not mean that England had become as yet the home of a general movement in favour of the "new learning." Many years were to elapse before the influence of these men was fully felt, and while the reign of Henry VII. is to be noted as a period which made its contribution to the growth of the new movement, it was not until the reign of Henry VIII. that the full effects of their work began to be felt. Even then the true renaissance was delayed, and if we seek the full flower of the new culture in England we have to move forward to a period outside the limits set for this book. Before the first steps could be taken much must happen. A generation had to pass away. Lawyers of the old school, like the father of Thomas More, remained hostile to the new ideas until the end, and the young enthusiast was set to study English law when he yearned for deeper acquaintance with classical literature. Perhaps the discipline was not without its advantages. English law, scholastic as it was in form, was a rich training-ground for logical thinking, and its stereotyped formalism only served to throw into high relief the contrast between the method and the content of scholastic and renaissance studies. Although More became a master of legal science, he never allowed his earlier enthusiasms to wane, and he stands as the symbol of that conflict between the old ideals and the new in which the victory, though it might be delayed, was bound to rest ultimately with the movement which had within itself the power to transform the world. The conservative instincts of Englishmen were not silenced in a night, and if the reign of Henry VII. saw the birth of an active renaissance school of thought, it must not be forgotten that time was to elapse before the full influence of its members was felt.

The second feature of the English renaissance movement which is worth a little emphasis is not the most spectacular, but it is of great importance. In 1499 Erasmus came to England, and the English humanists caught a first glimpse of one whom they were henceforth to reverence as their leader. Contemporaries could not have appreciated the deep importance of that visit, for the problem that it was to influence was not at that time in existence, but its meaning, in the light of history, is clear. When Martin Luther shook the world in 1519, he and Erasmus agreed about their objective, but they had fundamentally different views as to how that objective could best be reached. Each thought the other wrong, and so they were never able to join forces. The English humanists naturally tended towards the ideas of Erasmus, and the bias thus given to the renaissance movement in England had important results. For

74

when Lutheran ideals began to be preached English thinkers did not readily respond to them. The acceptance of such a statement does not imply the non-existence of Lutheran ideas in the England of Henry VIII. What it does mean is that when religious controversy became vocal the ideas which were expressed were in keeping with the ideas of Erasmus rather than of Luther, with the result that the English Reformation moved on different lines from those of the religious movements abroad. The importance of this Erasmian bias will best be appreciated when we come to study the characteristics of the religious changes of the reign of Henry VIII.

The third feature of the English renaissance is one which must be placed to the credit of Henry VII. Mediæval as he was in spirit, he was open to new influences, and he allowed his children to be given the benefit of the " new learning " that was reaching England. As a result, the next king was well trained for his office. He spoke French, Latin, Spanish, a little Italian. He played the lute and harpsichord. He sang, and composed ballads. He was an athlete. Perhaps there was a grain of truth in the later tradition that his father had intended Henry VIII. for office in the Church, but whether the tale be true or false, it is certain that he received a training that would not have disgraced an archbishop. Here again is a fact not to be overlooked in dealing with the English Reformation. In command of affairs was a monarch whose intellectual abilities were far from mean. He was the product of humanism, could take an intelligent and real interest in the religious problems of his age, and was able to direct the course of English thought and governmental policy to a degree that explains more clearly than anything else could do the unique quality of the Reformation movement in this country.

The attractive personalities of those who formed the group of English humanists tempt the historian to turn biographer, but that temptation must be resisted and attention must be concentrated upon the meaning of the movement in which the individuals were merged. For the essence of the renaissance was its challenge to the Church. From this point of view the attractive characters and the saintly lives of the leaders of the movement are of interest, for they stand out in striking contrast to the careless worldliness of many high ecclesiastics ; but the challenge was a wider one than this. It is to be found in the ideals of the humanists, and these in turn are to be sought in their actions rather than in any self-conscious manifestos of their ambitions. The true significance of the group of humanists lies not in the added lustre their presence gave to the court of Henry VIII., though this was great enough to draw from Erasmus a noteworthy panegyric. " You know, most excellent Bombasius," he says, " how I have always shrunk from the Courts of Princes, judging the life which is led there to be nothing but splendid misery, with a masquerade of happiness ; but into such a court as that [of England] one might well be pleased to remove, if youth could be recalled. The King, the most sensible monarch of our age, is delighted with good books, and the Queen is well instructed—not merely in comparison with her own sex—and is no less to be respected for her piety than her erudition. With such sovereigns, those persons have the greatest influence who excel in learning and in prudence. Thomas Linacre is their physician, a man whom it is needless for me to characterize when by his published books he has made himself sufficiently known. Cuthbert Tunstall is Master of the Rolls, an office which is of the highest dignity in that country, and when I name him, you cannot believe what a world of good qualities is implied. Thomas More is one of the Council, the supreme delight, not of the Muses only, but of Pleasantry and of the Graces, of whose genius you have been able to gain some scent from his books. Pace, with a character near akin, is the King's Secretary; William, Lord Mountjoy, is at the head of the Queen's household, and John Colet is the Preacher. I have only named the chief people. John Stokesley, who beside that scholastic Theology, in which he yields place to none, is also well versed in the Three Tongues, is one of the Chaplains. A palace filled with such men, may be called a Temple of the Muses rather than a Court. What Athens, what Porch, what Lyceum would you prefer to a Court like that ? " Such a group was more than an ornament. Its members had set themselves a great task, and it was in the performance of their self-imposed duty that they challenged the

Church, whose ideals and failures we have been examining.

The English renaissance naturally began as an enthusiastic reception of the Italian revival of classical culture. It never at any time ran the risk of ending—as much of the Italian enthusiasm had done—in a dilettante paganism. From the first, English scholarship had a strong Christian bias. Colet was inspired by the Italian humanists, More exaggerated the Christian piety of Giovanni Pico della Mirandola. Quite early the English humanists found a new view of the Christian Fathers, and their reverence for Erasmus naturally served to quicken their enthusiasm for these authorities whom he did so much to popularize. It is not meaningless that Colet's first appearance in public after his Italian wanderings was as a lecturer at Oxford on Paul's Epistle to the Romans, that Grocyn's sceptical mind toyed with the *Hierarchy* of Dionysius, that More's apprenticeship as a lecturer was served in the delivery of a course of lectures on St. Augustine's *City of God*. These subjects led naturally to theology and Church teaching. Colet was led inevitably to criticize the worldly Church, and his outspoken sermons brought large congregations to his church and consternation to the minds of ecclesiastics wise enough in their generation to read the signs of the times. Grocyn's inquiries caused him to stumble upon ecclesiastical pretensions which could not easily be substantiated. More's mind was turned from contemplation upon the *City of God* to the fashioning of an earthly

78

city unlike those he saw around him. His was a spirit nearly related to that of Erasmus. He had caught the trick of sly raillery characteristic of the author of the *Praise of Folly*. Like him, he knew how to hide ideas underneath whimsical jests whose seeming innocence made the satire no less deadly, and although the *Utopia* cannot be read as a book of which every word was written in deadly earnest, it has to be handled with the care which wise men reserve for high explosives.

The *Utopia* has become a classic, and its value as a guide to Tudor history need not be stressed. But it should be noticed that it is a forceful illustration of the Christian outlook of these English humanists. If its author looked forward to the possibilities of progress, he also looked backward with longing eyes to the ideals of the Middle Ages. Underneath the exaggerations of the *Utopia* there lies a whole philosophy of life. It crystallized into plain language ideas men were only beginning to recognize as the fundamental problems of the new age. It described and accounted for social and economic problems that were rapidly becoming grave realities of politics. It sensed the coming issues between Church and State, and while it garnered from the past the institutions and ideas worth preserving, it foretold and condemned the forces which would soon be making these the object of attack. The *Utopia* has many things to teach its readers even in these days, but its most devastating lesson was drawn from it by More's contemporaries. In 1535 Henry VIII. and his satellites were realizing that the man who had written such a book could not be on their side.

The work of the English humanists was practical. For them scholarship was a means to an end, and in their mouths the " new learning " became a gospel. For all their idealism they never lost sight of the dangers confronting their generation, and the solution of all problems they found in the word education. Colet voiced the prevailing discontent at the state of the Church in sermons like that preached before Convocation in 1512, but he had begun to see his way through the wood, and it was not the way of denunciation. " John Colet . . . desyring nothing more thanne Education and bringing vpp chyldern in good Maners and litterature in the yere of our Lorde a mli fyve hundreth and twelff bylded a Scole . . ." So begin the statutes for his foundation of St. Paul's School. It was the war-cry of the new movement. The spread of education and the destruction of superstition were the watchwords of the new age, and by the efforts of the humanists was begun a stimulus for the intellectual life of this country which was to have far-reaching results.

Such were some of the ideas gaining ground in England during the reign of Henry VII., and in the early years of the reign of his son. When they are compared with what has been said above concerning the ideals of the Christian Church, it will be seen that they do not stand out in violent contrast to the ideals which the Church at its best moments never ceased to represent. And yet, when they are thought of side by side with some of the failings of the fifteenth-century Church there can be few who would wish to deny the striking contrast presented. In that contrast lies more than half the English Reformation movement.

CHAPTER V

PERHAPS the most suggestive feature of the history of England from the death of Henry VII. until 1529 is that such history is rarely written. What is called the history of England for that period is really only the biography of one man. Here is something worth a pause, not because it represents a stereotyped method of writing history which we wish to pillory, but because it reveals a most illuminating truth. There is always a great deal to be said for fashions in historiography, and the feature to which attention has been drawn is sound proof of the importance of Thomas Wolsey in the life of his country. There is, however, a danger in the presentation of the history of those years as though they were nothing but the story of his life, and if this method is to be adopted, it should be prefaced with a warning. The multifarious variety of Wolsey's activities makes it difficult to control his biography, and in most of the accounts of him pride of place is given to his doings as a foreign minister, while the other aspects of his life-work are neglected. That in itself is a serious shortcoming. It is emphasized by another equally common tendency. So much

attention is usually given to the personal side of
his biography that England is often forgotten.
Now the really important problem is not what
Wolsey did or did not do, but what effect his com-
missions and omissions had upon his country ;
and neglect of England results in a misleading
view of the period. Thus two serious consequences have to be guarded against in a biographical interpretation of those years. For the
neglect of Wolsey's general activities omits the
most important part of his work, while emphasis
upon his foreign policy depicts that statesman not
—as is so often stated—at his best, but at his
weakest. And neglect of England breaks the
continuity of our national history, so that when the
student brought up on such methods comes to
study the English Reformation (which for him
will begin only in 1529), he fails to grasp the all-
important truth that during the twenty years
before that date a great deal was being accomplished without which the story of the Reformation is a meaningless puzzle.

Subject to these considerations the real approach
to English history in this period lies through
Wolsey. The astonishing virility and superb
intellectual equipment of the man enabled him
to tower above his generation like a Colossus.
In him the world saw a man who was a " maker
of history " to a degree not usually true of those
to whom that hackneyed phrase is applied. The
difficulty of dealing with him lies less in choosing
what to say about him and his work than in deciding what not to say. Whatever the decision

arrived at, it is certain that emphasis upon his diplomatic activities is likely to lead to misunderstanding. Only a realization of the almost superhuman tasks he gave himself in every field of life can bring his real greatness home to modern minds, while a balanced criticism of his influence can only be made when the range of his activities brings a spirit of toleration into the judgments passed. A real estimate of his importance does not depend on rows of dates, nor will it be attained by tabulating the details of his policy. It is in the cast of his mind and the traits of his character that the secret of his career will be found. Wolsey presents a problem not to be solved by the superficial treatment of his work which follows, but it is hoped that something said may suggest the lines along which a more detailed examination should run. Such suggestions, however, should rest on some definite materials, so it will be advisable to begin by mapping out some of the landmarks in his career.

There are occasions when a dozen dates epitomize the problems it takes as many volumes to solve, and Wolsey's life is one of them. This son of Robert Wolsey, an Ipswich grazier and wool-merchant, was born in 1472–3. It was 1515, however, before he had his feet firmly planted on the steps to fame. How he reached there calls for a story which tells of hard work, persevering place-hunting, and steady advancement. He had grown up while most children are learning how to play, and by the time he was fifteen he had kept his terms at Magdalen College, Oxford, had gained his degree, and the nickname—so he told his biographer, Cavendish—of the " boy-bachelor." By 1498 he was fellow and third bursar of his college. Next year he was senior bursar. Through the good offices of the Marquis of Dorset, whose sons he tutored, he was instituted into the living of St. Mary's Limington, in Somerset, in 1500. He did not vegetate in the country. By the end of 1501 he had become chaplain to Deane, archbishop of Canterbury and lord chancellor of England. The death of Deane in 1503 freed him to go as chaplain to Sir Richard Nanfan, the deputy lieutenant of Calais, and with this appointment his worldly career can at last be said to have been assured. Through Nanfan he became known at court, and by 1507 Wolsey was chaplain to Henry VII. Friendship with Fox, bishop of Winchester and lord privy seal, resulted in his employment upon diplomatic missions, and the reputation for efficiency earned in such work won him the deanery of Hereford before 1509. About that time preferments were falling thick upon him. By 1510 he was registrar of the most noble order of the Garter, and soon afterwards became canon and prebendary of St. George's Chapel at Windsor. We first hear of him in the King's council in 1511, and he seems to have won the confidence of the young king very soon. When Henry embarked upon the French war in 1512, Wolsey was entrusted with the work of organization for the expedition. Success again attended his work. By 1514 he had been made bishop of Lincoln, but soon after he had been consecrated news came of the poisoning at Rome of Bainbridge, archbishop of York, and Wolsey was chosen to fill his place. High as this office was, it was not the highest ecclesiastical dignity in England, and something more must be acquired before he could stand out as the superior of Warham, archbishop of Canterbury. In 1515, after some difficulty, Wolsey was made a cardinal of the Church of Rome, and his superiority was achieved. It was increased by his succession to Warham in the office of lord chancellor in the same year. Yet Wolsey was not satisfied. To complete his control over England, including Canterbury, he must be made a *Legatus a latere*—the deputy of the Pope in England. It was an honour not easily won from Rome, and although Wolsey was appointed, after prolonged negotiations, in 1518, he had to wait until 1524 before he was given the office for life. When it had been obtained his supremacy was unchallenged. . . .

By November 1530 the race had been run. The proud cardinal, whose word had shaped the policy of England and dominated the politicians of Europe, was dead, dishonoured, an outcast from the court where once his word was law. . . .

Such are the essentials of a life which must be understood if English history during this period is to have any meaning. Some of the implications of these facts may be followed out a little farther as a means of gaining insight into the reasons for Wolsey's importance. First and foremost it should be noticed that Wolsey was the product of Henry VII.'s system. He was a "new" man.

86

From that fact flowed some consequences essential to an explanation of his career. Being a " new " man, the favoured of the king, it followed that he had been chosen—as were all the new men—because of his ability, and the immediate future was to show that those who first brought him to the notice of the king had made no mistake. It is indeed wrong to speak of ability in Wolsey's case as though it implied that he met the standards required of all who sought to serve the king. In Wolsey ability approached at any rate to a form of genius, and his intellectual qualifications stand high in an age when such powers were of a high standard in those who surrounded the throne. The fact that he was a new man implied more than ability. It meant that his career would depend entirely on his devotion to duty. Here, too, Wolsey can hardly be judged by comparison with his contemporaries. He was never at fault. His desire was to make himself an indispensable servant. Throughout his career he feared the approach of any one who might, by sedulous devotion to the monarchy, endanger his own position as sole confidant of the royal mind. There can be little doubt that the motive force of his career was his own astounding ambition. But it should also be noticed that here was an occasion when ambition was best served by loyalty to a royal master, and Wolsey cannot be criticized for failure as a servant. From him there was forthcoming at all times a loyal devotion to the interests of his master, which equalled that received by any other Tudor monarch from any ministerial dependent. When the records of other Tudor ministers are remembered, it will be realized how high is the standard by which Wolsey's services can be judged.

It is probable that Wolsey's rise as a new man was responsible for another all-important characteristic. There was in him that exaggerated sense of his own importance, so often the sign of the self-made man. He had that strain of vulgarity which marks the *arriviste*. These peculiarities revealed themselves in his love of ostentatious display, his insistence on obsequious service from dependents and suitors, his zeal to figure as a collector of *objets d'art*, his extravagant delight in magnificent residences, his studied attention to his dress and personal appearance, and his love of pomp which amounted almost to an obsession. In the days of his greatness these unlovely traits of character became notorious. His arrogance increased with the growth of his power, and his anxiety to satisfy his extravagance made him greedy for the gifts which place-hunters were ready to lavish upon him. It will be well not to dismiss these weaknesses too lightly as the defects of the new man. There was policy behind them, and it was policy rich in results for this country. Something more than vanity prompted Wolsey's insistence on the pageantry of life. On the world in general, and on Henry VIII. in particular, it had an influence. Wolsey's example proved that authority increased with show of dignity, and Henry learned to apply to the divinity that hedges a monarch all the trappings of magnificence which hid the monarch from his people's eyes and enriched his sovereignty before the multitude who choose by show.

One final result of Wolsey's rise to greatness must be brought to mind. Wolsey was a new man, and no one knew better than he what that implied. It meant that he was responsible for the shaping of royal policy, but it meant also that he would be the scapegoat for that policy. In the days of his greatness, when things were running smoothly, it is probable that he gave little heed to the thought. All the same, the sinister event which had ushered in the reign of Henry VIII. lay behind him, and it was an ominous hint. Henry VII.'s policy had been successful, but unpopular. Empson and Dudley had paid for that unpopularity with their lives. Henry VIII.'s policy might become unpopular. If it did, Wolsey would just as surely be the sacrifice. The eventuality was uncertain, but about one thing there was no doubt. If there were to be unpopularity it would not be Henry VIII. who would suffer. The king would emerge with public sympathy unalienated, and, what is more important, he would reap all the advantages without any of the disadvantages of Wolsey's work. Here lies the explanation of much in Wolsey's career. Henry gave him the reins because it paid him so to do. It was true Tudor policy. It is, however, worthy of remark that after Henry had learned the mysteries of the high office to which he had been called he never again allowed any other minister to wield as much authority as Wolsey had been granted.

The next suggestive feature in Wolsey's career is the apparently simple one that he was an ecclesiastic. Here, too, he stands as the symbol of Henry VII.'s policy. The new man was being paid for his services, and the payment was made in the most economical way possible, by the lavish grants of benefices of which the list already given is by no means exhaustive. Wolsey was throughout his career an unblushing pluralist, and as such he illustrates a deplorable tendency of the times. It was followed by grave results. This habit of treating ecclesiastical preferment as a perquisite of statesmen fostered a spirit of secularism in the high religious offices. This, in turn, was reflected in the cynical indifference with which the ordinary man regarded ecclesiastical organization. Wolsey the ecclesiastic is the explanation of much in Wolsey the statesman. For him politics came first, and the interests of the Church second. Nor is that all that the fusion meant. Apart from the relative importance of affairs of State and Church, the very fact that in Wolsey the interests of both were combined has a deep significance. He was chancellor, and cardinal, and legate. In him the Pope came to England in a way that was rare in our history. Englishmen saw the real powers of the Papacy at close quarters, and if they did not grasp what that meant, Henry VIII. most certainly did.

When we come to examine Wolsey's policy in detail, we shall be lacking in a sense of values if we fail to realize that the importance of this man's career lies primarily in what he did to carry on

the domestic policy of Henry VII. As will be
seen later, his diplomatic work was brilliant in
conception, but its ultimate results were little
short of tragic. Despite consummate skill in the
working out of his high designs, Wolsey's foreign
policy was futile. It is in the tremendous impression he left on this country through the policy he
formulated at home, that his chief claim to consideration lies. With some of the schemes which
dominated that work we must now be concerned.

Through all Wolsey's policy there runs one
constant theme. All he did was done to reach
one goal, and in that objective itself there was
nothing that was new. Wolsey, like Henry VII.,
saw the secret of good government in a strong
central authority able to assert a control over
all disintegrating elements within the state. To
attain this supremacy all his efforts were directed,
and in everything he did he strove to magnify
the importance of the kingship as the central
control that was to be above all individuals and
all institutions. It was his ambition to make his
king greater even than Henry VII. had been, and
that policy of the founder of the dynasty, which had
directed an attack upon those who sought to win
advantages for themselves by keeping alive old
feuds and the spirit of lawlessness, found in Wolsey
an able supporter. It has sometimes been suggested that what he aimed at was his own advancement, that he sought to make himself a king in fact
if not in name, that his supremacy was gained
at the expense of the dignity of his royal master.
Such a simple explanation of his career is an in-

justice to so subtle a mind. That he was ambitious, self-seeking, confident of his own abilities, and jealous for advancement is sheer truth ; but when all these things have been said they only amount to this : that Wolsey was a statesman. No man goes far along the road of statescraft without the firm conviction that he is the only man with power to save the state, and it is by such a conviction that Wolsey is to be judged. He was the true new man, the servant of the state, and accusations of conspiracy on his part to usurp the royal authority must be discounted by the reflection that he is typical of the new school of ministers, who were prepared to sacrifice all in the service of the state machine. True, a foreign ambassador said about him, that he ruled both king and kingdom, that on the ambassador's first arrival in England Wolsey said to him, " His Majesty will do so and so," that later he went forgetting himself saying, " We shall do so and so," and later said, " I shall do so and so." True too, that the same observer reported to his own government that if it were necessary at any time to neglect either the king or the cardinal, it would be much better to pass over the king than the cardinal. These are only specimens of the accusations levelled against him by contemporary observers, but the *obiter dicta* of foreigners must be used with discrimination. Behind such impressions of Wolsey there lies a deeper truth. His autocratic bearing and unprecedented power were indisputable, but there was a reason for them, and it is a reason only to be found in the state

92

papers of the period. These show that Wolsey occupied his position for the very simple reason that the young king wished him to occupy it. The relations between master and servant were satisfactory to both. Wolsey never forgot that he had a master. He was always careful to explain to the king what he was doing. He laid state papers before him, wrote lengthy explanatory letters, shared his schemes with the king. In short, he was the ideal secretary, and it was because Henry knew that he could trust him that he gained his supreme influence over the young king. That harmony between king and minister meant much for Wolsey. It meant, as we shall see in a moment, infinitely more for Henry VIII. and the country over which he reigned.

It is natural to find that in the working out of his policy for the consolidation of royal power Wolsey concentrated his attention upon those evils which the work of Henry VII. had failed to eradicate. Strenuous as had been that monarch's efforts, the danger from the overmighty subject had not been completely removed. It still existed, but in a different form. Family feuds, the quarrels of great men, the oppression of the poor by the rich—these were no longer the signals for private war to anything like the extent that had been the case when Henry VII. first gave his mind to the problem. A subtler, more sinister evil had taken their place. The mighty subject had specialized in using the law for unlawful purposes, and under cover of litigation he was still able to gain his ends by the manipulation of the judicial machinery.

93

It was in dealing with these evils that Wolsey's work was specially valuable. As chancellor he was the king's chief minister, and he included among his functions a legal authority which enabled him to exert a powerful influence over the administration of law. His ideal was that which dominated all his work. Law was to be available for rich and poor alike. The overmighty subject was to be crushed, the authority of the crown was to be enforced through the courts; justice was to be efficient and cheap. Such aims meant the extension of the policy of Henry VII. Thus petitions to the chancellor received careful attention, and the poor found in Wolsey a powerful friend. For their help the court of requests, developed by Henry VII., was further strengthened, and in 1516-17 it was given a fixed place in the White Hall of the Palace of Westminster. To crush the overmighty subject the court of star chamber was reinforced in order to extend the work Henry VII. had begun. By regular attendance in that court, and by the increased dignity he gave it, Wolsey added very considerably to its power, and made the suppression of the disorders he was attacking a well-nigh accomplished fact. What he thought of this court is well expressed in one of his letters to the king : ". . . and for your realm, our Lord be thanked, it was never in such peace nor tranquillity ; for all this summer I have had nother of reyut (riot), felony, ne forcible entry, but that your laws be in every place indifferently ministered, without leaning of any manner. Albeit there hath lately, as I am informed, been a fray betwixt Pygot your serjeant and Sir Andrew Windsor's servants, for the seisin of a ward whereto both they pretend titles : in the which fray one man was slain. I trust at the next term to learn them law of the Star Chamber, that they shall ware how from thenceforth they shall redress their matter with their hands. They be both learned in the temporal law, and I doubt not good example shall ensue to see them learn the new law of the Star Chamber, which, God willing, they shall have indifferently ministered to them according to their deserts."

All this was to the good, and on the whole the reforms were popular ; but such work made Wolsey feared by the great, and he was one day to learn that fear forms fruitful soil for hate. The literature of the time suggests the passion to which his work gave rise, and Skelton's poetry, though undoubtedly the fruit of prejudice, is an interesting illustration of the fury of Wolsey's opponents. The works of this poet are not well known, and a specimen may be useful as a gauge of the literary forms as well as the political opinions of the time. It depicts Wolsey at work as a judge.

> " Juges of the kynges lawes,
> He countys them foles and dawes ;
> Sergyantes of the coyfe eke,
> He sayth they are to seke
> In pletynge of theyr case
> At the Commune Place,
> Or at the Kynges Benche ;
> He wryngeth them suche a wrenche,
> That all our lerned men
> Dare nat set theyr penne

To plete a trew tryall
Within Westmynster hall :
In the Chauncery where he syttes,
But suche as he admyttes
None so hardy to speke ;
He sayth, thou huddypeke,
Thy lernynge is to lewde,
Thy tongue is nat well thewde,
To seke before our grace ;
And openly in that place
He rages and he raues,
And cals them cankerd knaues :
Thus royally he dothe deale
Vnder the kynges brode seale ;
And in the Checker he them cheks ;
In the Ster Chambre he noddis and beks,
And bereth him there so stowte,
That no man dare rowte,
Duke, erle, baron, nor lorde,
But to his sentence must accorde ;
Whether he be knyght or squyre
All men must follow his desyre."

Wolsey had only himself to blame for the hate he inspired. His success was in part the result of his arrogance, but it was bought at a price, as his subsequent downfall was to show. In proof of that arrogance much evidence could be produced, but one representative illustration of Wolsey in action as chancellor must suffice. It will be found in the first biography of the cardinal, that written by Cavendish some time before 1577. " Now will I declare unto you his order in going to Westminster Hall daily in the term season. First, before his coming out of his privy chamber, he heard most commonly every day two masses in his privy closet ; and there

then said his daily service with his chaplain : and
as I heard his chaplain say . . . the cardinal,
what business or weighty matters soever he had
in the day, he never went to his bed with any part
of his divine service unsaid, yea not so much as
one collect : wherein I doubt not but he deceived
the opinion of divers persons. And after mass he
would return in his privy chamber again, and
being advertized of the furniture of his chambers
without, with noblemen and gentlemen, and other
persons, would issue out into them, apparelled all
in red, in the habit of a cardinal ; which was
either of fine scarlet, or else of crimson satin,
taffety, damask, or caffa, the best that he could
get for the money : and upon his head a round
pillion, with a nekke of black velvet set to the
same in the inner side ; he had also a tippet of
fine sables about his neck ; holding in his hand a
very fair orange, whereof the meat or substance
within was taken out, and filled up again with the
part of a sponge, wherein was vinegar and other
confections, against the pestilent airs ; to the
which he most commonly smelt unto, passing
among the press, or else when he was pestered
with many suitors. There was also borne before
him first, the Great Seal of England, and then his
cardinal's hat, by a nobleman or some worthy
gentleman, right solemnly, bareheaded. And as
soon as he was entered into his chamber of
presence, where was attending his coming to await
upon him to Westminster Hall, as well noblemen
and other worthy gentlemen, as noblemen and
gentlemen of his own family : thus passing forth

97

with two great crosses of silver borne before him ; with also two great pillars of silver, and his pursuivant at arms with a great mace of silver gilt. Then his gentlemen ushers cried, and said : ' On, my lords and masters ; make way for my Lord's Grace ! ' Thus passed he down from his chambers through the hall ; and when he came to the hall door, there was attendant for him, his mule, trapped all together in crimson velvet, and gilt stirrups. When he was mounted, with his cross bearers, and pillar bearers, also upon great horses trapped with red scarlet, then marched he forward, with his train and furniture in manner as I have declared, having about him four footmen with gilt poleaxes in their hands ; and thus he went until he came to Westminster Hall door. And there lighted, and went after this manner, up through the hall into the chancery ; howbeit he would most commonly stay a while at a bar, made for him, a little beneath the chancery on the right hand, and there commune some time with the judges, and some time with other persons. And that done, he would repair into the chancery, sitting there until eleven of the clock, hearing suitors, and determining of divers matters. And from thence he would divers times go into the Star Chamber, as occasion did serve : when he spared neither high nor low, but judged every estate according to their merit and deserts."

This majestic bearing was not reserved exclusively for suitors at law. In all transactions Wolsey's attitude was imperious. Ambassadors complained of his ruthless neglect of ceremony towards them, and the autocratic manner in which he conducted negotiations. The aristocracy objected to his supercilious attitude towards them. Even parliament was moved to anger at his studied insolence in dealing with it.

This last indictment ought to be considered as a potential rather than an actual source of trouble to Wolsey, for those to whom that institution is the dominant feature of our constitution will find it difficult to understand early Tudor history unless they learn to think of parliament as only slowly coming to a position of importance during those years. Under Henry VII. it was only summoned on seven occasions, and it was not consulted on the real issues which arose during the reign. That tradition was continued by Wolsey, who persistently regarded it merely as a machine to be used in order to extract pledges for taxation. His attitude was frankly hostile. It was by his advice that the parliament of 1515 was dissolved, and during the period when he was supreme, only one parliament—that of 1523—was called. With that assembly he was soon embroiled in a dispute over a money grant. The fact is significant, for it suggests one of Wolsey's greatest difficulties. His ambitious policy at home and abroad cost money, and the parliament of 1523 only met to solve the question of ways and means. Wolsey's methods were the reverse of tactful, and although in the end the crown was granted a subsidy, it was not given in the form Wolsey had designed, nor did his dictatorial manner improve his personal

99

position in the eyes of members and of the subjects they were representing.

This incident is a reminder that no description of Wolsey's régime would be adequate without a mention, however cursory, of the subject of finance. The complexities of his foreign policy, military activities, and reckless expenditure, left on his hands an ever-present task of raising supplies, and the unpopularity with which the country heard his demands made it essential for him to employ expedients whereby funds could be raised without giving parliament an opportunity to voice protests. Not the least remarkable of Wolsey's administrative achievements were those connected with finance, but the intricacies of the subject do not permit of more than a bare suggestion of his policy. It must be enough to state that by 1525 Wolsey had grappled with the question of household expenditure, and had adopted plans for raising the supplies necessary for the work of government by schemes meriting considerable credit. His economies and his reorganization within the royal household made for efficiency, but—this was of vital importance—they cost him popularity he could ill afford to lose amongst those courtiers who found that the new regulations robbed them of sinecures and the perquisites of offices which attendance at court had brought into their hands.

The cardinal's position as a high ecclesiastic made it impossible for him to be without an influence, be it only negative, upon the Church in England. And his influence was far removed from negative. The man who was the papal representative in this country could not fail to be a significant figure in the inter-relation of Church and State, and any one whose eyes are beginning to stray towards the years after 1529 must be wondering what influence is going to be ascribed to the rule of Wolsey upon questions that would soon be fundamental issues in a bitter fight.

The statesman Wolsey had little time for active interest in the " new learning," and there is little to be said about him as a participator in the English humanist movement. Even so, it stands to his credit that he did at any rate appreciate the conflict between new and old. In the party divisions which were forming he may quite fairly be placed in the ranks of those who realized that the changing spirit of the age was full of peril for the Church unless its leaders stirred themselves. The insistence on efficiency so characteristic of all he did, betrayed itself in his ecclesiastical work, and in the policy he formulated for the organization of the Church he was inspired more by a desire for better government than by scruples of morality. The blemishes in his own character were such as would have made him a hypocritical reformer of the lives of other men, but in the reorganization of Church government he was as full of plans as he was in all other branches of his work, and his reforms were effective. The authority he possessed gave him ample powers to introduce such measures. *Legatus a latere*, he wielded unquestionable power as a papal representative, and under his rule churchmen and laymen alike learned what such authority might imply. The insularity of England had always helped to keep the Pope at bay. In Wolsey's time men realized what powers the Holy Father could assert, and the future was to show that such knowledge was not as beneficial to the Pope as at first sight it might have seemed to be.

Wolsey's plans were not revolutionary. He was no reformer in the sense that that word was to imply a little later, but his policy reveals his realist conception of the state of English religious life. The spirit of worldliness, the lack of morality, the failure of the Church to perform those functions which history and human needs expected of her, were the starting-point from which his plans progressed. His ideal for the English Church was the destruction of ignorance and lax discipline, the thorough reorganization of ecclesiastical government, and the control of the Church in the interests of the sovereign he was doing so much to serve.

His reformation work is the story of the acquisition of powers sufficient to enable him to make his influence felt. It began with control over the religious orders, and in 1519 he issued regulations based partly on earlier papal legislation, and partly on his own schemes for the reform of the Augustinian orders. Reform of the Benedictines was undertaken in 1524, and in the next year the cardinal turned his attention to the Dominican Friars. They seem to have been prepared to submit, but the Grey Friars were less passive, and their dislike of his schemes led to their becoming a source of annoyance to him. This control was accompanied by the assertion of supremacy over the Church in general. In 1518 Wolsey held a visitation for St. Paul's Cathedral, bringing order into an establishment where financial disorganization was reacting seriously on discipline. In 1528 he obtained from the Pope special powers for dealing with criminous clerks, and in the administration of Church courts—especially those of Arches and Audience—he tried to carry on the legal reforms which had marked his work in other fields.

Such reforms did not exhaust Wolsey's desires, but they were a beginning. If he had devoted more of his attention to such questions he would have done work that might have altered the whole course of future religious history. His ideas on Church reform did not end with the regulation of abuses. However unimportant the name of Wolsey in the history of the English renaissance, one thing is certain : he was not slow to see that the ideas of the new movement would have to be applied to the Church, and the best known of his religious projects is that by which he tried to bring the " new learning " into the Church. He realized that the secret of efficient clergy lay in education, and he strove to turn his ideal into practical politics. His relations with Oxford were close enough to allow him to work there, and the foundation of lectureships in theology, civil law, physics, philosophy, mathematics, Greek, and rhetoric, marked a beginning. But he had more spacious dreams. He visualized a means of supplying the Church with well-educated clergy. A school at Ipswich (his native place) was to be the fountain from which an Oxford college could draw its supplies. The school never matured, for after Wolsey's fall it was completely destroyed ; the college—credit for which Henry VIII. annexed—in part survived in the foundation of Christ Church. Such plans as Wolsey was entertaining were not feasible without funds, and the methods whereby he set about acquiring them, though defensible, were full of danger for the future. Inspired by the knowledge that there existed in England religious houses in which earlier ideals of discipline and usefulness were languishing, Wolsey argued that they had outlived their generation. After much negotiation he obtained papal permission to dissolve such of them as contained only six members. The proceeds were to be used for his Oxford college and Ipswich school. In a similar spirit he used his powers as visitor to some of the bigger foundations in order to frighten them, and the money gifts they offered in order to propitiate him were spent in the same work. Such plans, beneficial as they might have become, aroused considerable opposition, and in the day of reckoning these good works told as heavily against Wolsey as did the less reputable practices of which he was accused.

Enough has been said by way of illustration of Wolsey's ecclesiastical policy. It represents, after all, only a part of his activities. His real importance lies in the cumulative effect of these varied interests upon life in the England of his day, and the sole object gained by bringing together these facts is the realization of the results of his activity upon his country. Before such an estimate can be made, something must be said upon another sphere of his work.

It is difficult to follow the arguments of those whose praise of Wolsey's foreign policy is unqualified. It is true that his policy, spectacular as it was, stands out in striking contrast to the unheroic carefulness of Henry VII.'s schemes, but diplomacy has to be measured by a more definite test than its dramatic effects. It is possible to argue that more lay beneath Wolsey's schemes than this mere appeal to the imagination; that his policy did mean the rise of England in the European world; that as a result of it this country was able to hold the balance of European diplomacy, so that the scales could be moved in accordance with Wolsey's desires; that England in consequence became a power whose alliance was eagerly sought after by France and Spain; and that Wolsey's personal influence in Europe became so great that twice—in 1521 and 1523— his name was being canvassed for the papal chair. All these things are at any rate arguable, but before any conclusion can be arrived at concerning the value of his achievements, there is a fundamental question to be answered. What did these things really mean for England? It may or may not be true that during Wolsey's rule this country became the arbiter in European politics, but the important issue is whether such a result was worth the efforts it cost. It may be that Wolsey became the supreme figure in European diplomacy, but the vital thing for England was, could he make European rulers do what England wanted them to do ? It is possible that the cardinal almost became a Pope, but was there at any moment any real hope of bridging that " almost," and did Wolsey's foreign policy help or hinder his attainment of the high office he sought ? These are the questions to be pondered before a full criticism of his work can be made, and when his foreign policy is looked at from the viewpoint such questions suggest, it will not be found easy to subscribe to some of the panegyrics written on his work. Throughout the whole period when he held office Wolsey was actively engaged in weaving the web of an intricate diplomatic policy, but the impression left on any critical mind is that much of the activity was illusory, and that Wolsey's schemings ultimately ended in worse than nothing. The reality of this view will best be brought out by a more detailed glance at his work.

In the first of the periods into which the foreign policy of his reign naturally falls—covering the years from 1509 to 1515—Henry VIII. (using a well-filled treasury and indulging a rivalry with France which England's traditional hostility supported and Spain's policy encouraged) embarked on a war with that country. Its sole result was to show Henry and the world how unimportant England really was. Ferdinand, having won Navarre, deserted his son-in-law and made his peace with France. It was this débâcle which gave Wolsey his first chance in diplomacy, and he made first-rate use of it. It was soon clear that in him England had a diplomat who could beat Ferdinand's low cunning. By a brilliant stroke Wolsey warded off the ill effects of Ferdinand's treachery by arranging, in 1514, a marriage between Louis XII. of France and Mary, sister of Henry VIII. The French king agreed to increase the payments his country was making to England as a result of the peace of Etaples, and England and France went into the future as allies. Wolsey had made a good beginning, but it was fated to be nothing more. By January 1515 Louis XII. was dead. All the advantages of the marriage were lost ; the widow Mary was a problem for the governments of England and France : all Wolsey's work had to be begun over again.

In the phase from 1515–18 much of the cardinal's policy was elaborately subtle and expensive, for it meant the financing of the Emperor Maximilian in order to prevent the growth of France after the successful Italian campaign which had culminated in the battle of Marignano, September 13, 1515. But it was not altogether unjustified, and with the papal attempt of 1517 to persuade Europe to undertake a crusade against the Turk, Wolsey had an opportunity which was the high-water mark of his achievements. The treaty of universal peace which he manœuvred in 1518 must not be taken seriously. Its real value lay not in the hope of a cessation of hostilities between the turbulent European states, but in the added prestige which it gave England and Wolsey. It made the cardinal the centre of European diplo-

macy and the arbiter of European affairs. Any
optimistic views of its effect upon the question of
world peace were abruptly destroyed by the death
of Maximilian in 1519. Instantly Europe was in
a ferment, and the keen rivalry of Charles of Spain
and Francis of France for election to the Empire
formed the paramount problem of continental
politics.

The phase from 1519–27 was the period when
Wolsey's ideas for holding a balance in foreign
policy had the fullest scope ; but the results were
little short of disastrous. Both France and Spain
were eager rivals for an English alliance, and
Wolsey had a clear field. His elaborate duplicity
at the Field of Cloth of Gold in 1520 deceived no
one, least of all the French king, with whom the
conference was being held ; and the alliance in
1521 with Charles of Spain, who had now become
emperor, threw England definitely on one side in
the party division of Europe. It was a decision
of great moment. It led England into an unpopular war with France, alienated what sympathy
still remained to Wolsey in England, encouraged
the Scots in their anti-English intrigues, and
reacted upon the Eastern menace by enabling the
Turk to advance farther into Europe. More important still was the fact that it gave the Emperor
Charles the opportunity he wanted. As a result
of England's refusal to join Francis, he became
the successful rival of France in Italy. His resources enabled him to inflict a crushing defeat on
Francis at Pavia in 1525, and he was encouraged
by his successes to aim at a domination in Europe.

So powerful did he become that, when he found his policy hampered by the schemings of the Pope, he even went so far as to sack the city of Rome in 1527. Here was a new phase in the long rivalry of Empire and Papacy. In any circumstances it would have been spectacular; under the conditions then obtaining it was of vital importance. The effect of the sack of Rome was that it made Pope Clement VII. little better than a puppet in the hands of Charles. What England obtained as a result of Wolsey's plans will best be seen when we have gone a little further in her history. For the present it is enough to notice that neither English interests nor the more personal ambitions of Wolsey himself had gained anything by support of Spain, for the emperor was now dominant in Europe, and he had done nothing to carry out his promises to support Wolsey's candidature to the Papacy.

Meanwhile the cardinal was hampered by a factor which was a striking comment on the failure of his work. The fierce problem of Henry VIII.'s marriage to, and estrangement from, Catherine of Aragon cannot be separated from the many questions giving the reign its interest. The events connected with it make a dark stain that spreads across the history of the period. It was to give rise to great difficulties, and a full discussion of it will be best appreciated if reserved for another place. It cannot be altogether ignored in an estimate of Wolsey's life and work, for when the question became one of practical politics, in 1527, it presented a puzzle which made Wolsey's foreign policy impossible. The complications were enormous. The annulment of Henry's marriage could only be arranged by the Pope. The result of Wolsey's diplomacy had been, as we have seen, to place the Pope in the hands of Charles V. The emperor was the nephew of Catherine. Thus the policy of juggling with the idea of balance had led by 1527 to this astonishing result. Wolsey had forced the king's judge into the arms of the king's opponents. He did his best to undo the mischief by attempting to destroy the preponderancy of Spain by alliance with France. But the work of earlier years could not be undone in a moment, while the king's " secret matter " could not wait. Wolsey was caught as though in a trap. In a short time all those who hated him were taking advantage of his difficulties, and the king, far too eager to gain the satisfaction of his personal desires, sacrificed one who had spent his life in faithful service. By November 1530 Cardinal Wolsey was no more.

The tragic pathos of Wolsey's fall, and moralizings on the ingratitude of monarchs to those who serve them best, must not blind us to the more constructive results of Wolsey's work. Everything he had done was not buried in his tomb, and the real significance of his life-work will not be seen unless the fragments which survived are examined. What such a study is likely to show is that Wolsey's importance lies less in what he did—great as that was—than in what he taught others to do. He stands out in Tudor history as an ominous figure, for he spoke the prologue to the Tudor " despotism." The effects of his work upon the people of England were mixed. On the one hand, men saw the advantages derived from efficient government, which had as its aims the administration of law and the defence of the poor against the rich, the weak against the strong. There is reason to think that the majority were not disposed to grudge the price that they were called upon to pay for such benefits. And so the way was being prepared for the full development of royal power. On the other hand, Wolsey's high ecclesiastical status helped to suggest to the minds of men another idea. They were tempted to transfer their dislike of his autocracy to the Church he represented, and there was fostered a spirit which will be worth remembering when the time comes for us to take a glance at the religious history of succeeding years.

It was, however, upon the king that Wolsey's example had an influence that was permanent and almost incalculable. Henry's debt to his minister was greater than he ever knew. The statesman had trained the king in habits of statesmanship, had shown him how policy was developed, had helped him to learn the many secrets of his high place. There would have been a Henry VIII. if there had been no Wolsey ; he would have been a man of alert intelligence and considerable native ability, but he would have lacked that grasp of affairs, that capacity for concentrating on the details of policy, and that sane, shrewd judgment of issues which Wolsey instilled into him in the years of training. Through Wolsey Henry learned many things. He learned what to do. He learned also—and this was perhaps of even greater moment —what to avoid. He saw the possibilities inherent in ostentatious display of power and wealth, because he saw how they succeeded with Wolsey. He learned how a show of dignity could capture the public imagination, and how it might be used to create a form of government that might almost be despotic. But he learned, too, the terms on which alone such a form of government would be allowed. It would have to be efficient. It must be exercised with tact. Wolsey's lack of this gift, and, above all, his mistakes in dealing with parliament, taught Henry the most vital lesson of all. He saw that if he was to be really successful he must cultivate that institution. Wolsey's failure was the stepping-stone for Henry's success. All these things were implicit in his career, but perhaps the greatest of the lessons Henry learned from his minister was that which came from Wolsey's unique position. In him were combined the powers of the ecclesiastic and the statesman. The legate was the deputy of a pope ; the chancellor was the deputy of a king. With the powers accruing from the two he carried all before him. It needed less of a logician than Henry VIII. to follow out the argument to its conclusion. It is no mere accident that Wolsey's fall marks the beginning of the attempt to reach a greater ideal. Was it not possible that what the minister had been the master might become ? Might not the king be also a pope—the supreme head of the Church be also the sovereign lord in the State ? To think of such things in Wolsey's day might have been the wildest day-dream ; but such was the legacy he bequeathed to his king, that we shall find ourselves discussing them as stern realities in the next chapter.

CHAPTER VI

REFORM

THE real hindrance to an understanding of the
English Reformation is that which comes
from a failure to appreciate the amount of
history being made in England in a short period
of time. To this must be added another difficulty. It needs close concentration to realize how
various incidents, which, taken separately, seem
to have little or nothing in common, combined to
form the problem under discussion. The issue
may be stated more definitely. The vital years in
the history of the Reformation may be spoken of
in round numbers as those from 1527 to 1537.
Suppose we look at them a little more closely. Is
it easy to realize their full import? In 1527
Wolsey was learning that his king had grave doubts
about the legality of his marriage to Catherine,
who had been his brother's wife, and whose
marriage to Henry had only been possible by the
grant of a papal dispensation authorizing such a
union within the forbidden degrees. In ten years
those doubts had led to changes which transformed a nation. They had ruined Wolsey's plans
and sent him to an unhonoured grave. They had
drawn Henry into a conflict with the Pope, had

114

caused him to defy ecclesiastical authority, separate from his wife, marry Anne Boleyn, make her his queen and the mother of his child, behead her, and take another wife. On the other hand, those same doubts had put the Pope in serious difficulties, causing him to pursue for years a policy of unsystematic intrigue which only served to make his difficulties greater. They had made him curse the day when Henry and Catherine brought their difficulties before him, had caused him to threaten Henry, and—when he saw the futility of threats—had caused him to put into operation against him, whom once he called Fidei Defensor, the final judgment of the Church on earth. In 1535 Henry VIII. was excommunicated.

Such incidents provide a narrative which is large enough for any average ten years of history. In themselves the facts are not very remarkable. Henry VIII. was not the first sovereign, not even the first English king, to defy a Pope, nor was he the first to be excommunicated. The stupendous significance of those years is only brought home to the mind when it is remembered that he was the first English monarch who could afford to be completely indifferent to the anathemas of Rome. Unless we knew the reason why, we should find it hard to guess. Henry could be indifferent to the Pope because he himself had become a kind of Pope in England. That it was even possible for such a proposal to be made should be enough to suggest our difficulties. For here is something that could not have been gleaned from what has been already said. The crowded years which

witnessed the events already mentioned possess
other secrets ; and these have to be brought into
the narrative before the puzzle of the English
Reformation is complete. This fresh material
which has to be dealt with is in some ways the
most difficult of all to understand. It consists
almost exclusively of acts of parliament.

Between 1529 and 1536 an English parliament
had been sitting—in sessions of varying length—
and its members had seen an astonishing amount
of legislation pass through their hands. Bare
enumeration of the statutes by their titles would
make lengthy and dreary reading, but fortunately
it is possible to look at them in a more profitable
way. For that series of acts, whether viewed in
order of time or of importance, falls naturally into
several groups which are very definitely parts of
one logical policy. As a consideration of that
policy is indispensable to an understanding of the
Reformation, it is essential to differentiate between
the motives which can be discerned behind each
group.

All the statutes to be considered have one thing
in common—they are all, directly or indirectly,
concerned with the Church. The groups into
which they fall will best show what place they have
in the general scheme. There are, first of all,
those acts which attacked abuses connected with
the privileges enjoyed by the Church in England.
In the second group are those which warned the
English clergy they must acquiesce in what was
being done. The third group consists of acts
which dealt with the bigger problem of the re-

lationship between the Church in England and the Church catholic with its head at Rome. In the fourth are the acts which aimed at some measure of reconstruction after the destructive attacks made by some of the statutes in the other groups. Now the bulk of the material relevant to the English Reformation, so far as that movement went in the reign of Henry VIII., will be found to be connected in some way with this legislation, and before it is possible to discuss the wider implications of the movement, some of the objectives at which this legislation of the Reformation Parliament was aimed must be examined.

The first problem dealt with was that suggested by the statutes in the first group mentioned, which attacked some of the privileges enjoyed by the Church in England. They did not attempt to deal with all, but they made an important start by attacking those abuses which were most directly felt, and were therefore most unpopular. These acts were, therefore, certain of a fairly general support. The Probate and Mortuaries Acts of 1529 met the Church on its own ground, for they dealt with the business arrangements consequent upon death. Extortionate demands made by the clergy for the performance of duties they alone were privileged to perform were checked. A fixed tariff was made for payments due for the administratio.. of wills and for mortuary fees. By the Pluralities Act, 1529, another flagrant abuse of the times was attacked, by establishing the principle (with some exceptions) that any clergyman holding a benefice of the value of £8 a year or more was to vacate it when he accepted another living. Non-residence of the clergy was an evil from which much of the dissatisfaction with the Church at this period derived its inspiration, and popular support was certain to be forthcoming for legislation to put an end to this abuse. Church jurisdictional privileges had led, as was shown earlier, to grave evils. In 1531 the serious menace from sanctuary rights and the privilege of benefit of clergy, which had already been partially dealt with by Henry VII., was again considered. Benefit of clergy was severely restricted, a rigid definition being laid down of the qualifications necessary to obtain the privilege, while abjuration of the realm was abolished and sanctuary rights were more closely defined. It should be realized that such legislation dealt with obvious defects in Church organization, abuses which were responsible for much of the dissatisfaction with which many minds of the time were exercised. These efforts to remedy the evils interested the country, and the priority of time which was given to them in the transactions of this parliament enlisted popular support on the side of the king in preparation for the more drastic policy he already had in view.

Signs of the coming of these wider problems will be found in the legislation assigned to the second group of statutes. They must be interpreted in the light of an act of 1393 called the Statute of Præmunire. Stated briefly, that act allowed a writ called Præmunire to be issued against any one who brought into England any

papal letters or sentences of excommunication
or other documents which affected the position
of the king, his royalty or his realm. In October
1529 this act was used against Wolsey, and in
December 1530 the threat which had ended
Wolsey's career as a statesman was applied to the
clergy generally. The charge against Wolsey had
been that he had incurred the penalties of præmunire through the exercise of his office as legate,
and now the clergy were placed under the same
penalties for their recognition of him in this office.
This recognition they had shared with the king
himself, for Henry had done his utmost to get
Wolsey appointed, and had licensed his appointment when it was made. Henry was not the man
to quibble over nice questions of this kind when
his own plans were being worked out. The
penalties now threatened meant forfeiture of
goods and imprisonment, and whatever language
may be used to describe the cunning trick of which
Henry was guilty, there can be no doubt of its
success. It frightened the clergy. In 1531 the
clergy of the province of Canterbury bought their
pardon from the king by a payment of £100,000.
In 1532 those of the province of York paid
£18,840, 0s. 10d. for theirs. The state of feeling
in parliament and the country generally may be
judged from the fact that members were not willing
to pass the act for the pardon of the clergy of
Canterbury as it stood, because it only applied
to ecclesiastics. They argued that all persons,
lay as well as clerical, who had recognized the
cardinal were equally liable to the penalties

119

mentioned. So another act, pardoning the laity for such offences, was also passed. Henry's pardon to the laity was symbolic. It was given freely.

With the clergy thus cowed, the way was open for the third group of acts, which were more definitely attacks upon the Church catholic and its head. As early as 1532 parliament gave Henry a weapon for use in his struggle with the Pope over the question of the annulment of his marriage. It took the form of an act in restraint of the payment to Rome of one year's whole profits of a spiritual preferment, a payment known as annates. The king was authorized by this act to compound for such payments, and was instructed to declare by Easter 1533 whether or not the act was to be put into force. There was another sinister clause which set up a provisional machinery for the consecration of archbishops and bishops without letters from Rome. The importance of this legislation lies in the motive behind it. It was meant for diplomatic purposes. It was intended to be a hint to the Pope of the retaliatory measures that would be taken if he did not meet the king's wishes with regard to the marriage question. The Pope did not take the hint, and the act was enforced by another in 1534. Similar legislation will be found in the Act in Restraint of Appeals, 1533, but it went to further extremes. For this act denied that the state was subject to any external power, be it temporal or spiritual, and it established the principle that spiritual causes—those concerning wills, marriages, tithes, and the like—were for the future to be heard in England.

When the Act in Restraint of Annates was passed in 1534 another statute accompanied it and forbade the payment of Peter's Pence to Rome, while the archbishop of Canterbury was authorized (for fixed payments) to issue dispensations which had previously been granted from Rome.

The most famous of the acts of this parliament fall, however, into the last group to be mentioned here. They may well be called constructive, for they attempt to state the logical conclusion of the legislation which was modifying the jurisdictional rights of the Church in England, and was cutting the English Church away from the control of the Papacy. Such legislation necessarily entailed some considered statement of the new position in which the clergy of this country found themselves, and some indications of the direction in which they were to look for leadership and control in the future. The avowed motive underlying the changes taking place was the desire to emphasize the control of the State over the Church. It was therefore evident whence the solution of this problem might be expected to come. Clear evidence was provided in the first important act that has a bearing on the subject. The Act for the Submission of the Clergy (1534) put into statutory form the submission won from the clergy in convocation in 1532, while it established royal control over the Church by enacting that the clergy should not for the future make any constitutions in convocation unless that assembly had first obtained royal permission so to do. This was important, but it was not as far-reaching as the

Act of Supremacy (1534), which has been well described as the "ornamental coping-stone which Henry placed upon his ecclesiastical policy." The act declared that the king was to be accepted as the only supreme head on earth of the Church of England. There was to be united to his royal dignity both the title and the honours, jurisdictions, and privileges pertaining to the said dignity of supreme head, and the king who wielded such powers was to have the right of reforming all errors, heresies, and abuses within the Church. In possession of such powers Henry was virtually Pope in England.

The royal supremacy which had been thus established had to be further strengthened. The same year which saw the Act of Supremacy passed, saw also some legislation regulating the succession to the crown. It was necessary because of the marriage of Henry and Anne Boleyn, and this Act of Succession of 1534 was the first of a series of attempts to settle a problem which owed its existence to the refusal of the Papacy to recognize the annulment of Catherine's marriage. By this act the marriage with Catherine was declared annulled, and the succession was vested in the heirs of the king and Anne Boleyn, while it was made a treasonable offence to criticize, either by writing or action, the marriage between the king and Anne. It may be stated here that this legislation was not enough to solve the succession problem, and when further complications made it necessary, fresh legislation for the purpose had to be made. This will have to be dealt with in another place. It is sufficient for our present purpose to realize that everything that was possible was being done to render the supremacy achieved in the legislation of 1534 unquestionable and permanent.

With the Acts for the Submission of the Clergy, the Act of Supremacy, and the Act for the Succession, the complement to the destructive attacks upon Church jurisdiction and the establishment of the unrivalled autocracy of the sovereign had been achieved. Henry was indeed king of England. The monarch upon whom his astonished subjects gazed in awe was such as neither they nor any of their ancestors had ever seen.

Only by marshalling in this way some of the main facts that went to make the history of England in the period between 1527 and 1537 can materials be gained for answering some of the questions without which the English Reformation is unintelligible. Immediately one question above all others leaps to the mind. It is one which leads us back to the point from which this chapter started, for the issue it raises is the nature of the link between the doubts about Henry's first marriage and the state of affairs in England about 1537. There is no special merit in being able to see that there was some connection between the efforts to get an annulment of Henry's first marriage and the Act of Succession of 1534, or in concluding that the so-called divorce had its influence upon the destinies of the English Church not merely in the reign of Henry VIII., but for all time. What does call for careful thought, however, is the exact character of that relationship.

What is difficult to estimate is the precise emphasis that ought to be placed upon the marriage problem as a factor in the English Reformation. Such a question is not an academic one, for even to-day—despite, or perhaps because of, all that has been written on the subject—the Reformation is a difficult problem which is not always studied in its proper perspective, and the interaction of the many influences at work is not as clearly borne in mind as it should be. After all, it makes some difference in the ultimate conclusions to be reached whether estimates are based on the view that the English Reformation, with all its political and ecclesiastical implications, was the direct result of Henry VIII.'s personal desires and ambitions, or on the more historical retrospect which sees behind the workings of a mortal man the surge of movements over which his will could have but small control.

How incomplete is the explanation which ascribes the changes of those years to Henry's personal and unattractive aims is best appreciated if we think of two suggestive arguments. The first of them is the indisputable one that throughout the controversies of the period public opinion on the whole was most decidedly in favour of Queen Catherine. From first to last the shadow of that tragic Spanish princess lay across the path Anne Boleyn desired to tread. Not only did the upstart rival fail to capture public sympathy, she was often in danger of hostile demonstrations when she appeared in public. Her tragic fate was looked upon in England as a grisly moral

summing up an evil tale. Yet, despite their
sympathy for Catherine, in face of bitter hostility
to Anne Boleyn, the English people acquiesced
in the changes which broke Catherine's heart,
and accepted with every appearance of approval
the actions to which Henry was driven as a result of his sordid intrigue. The acquiescence is
deeply suggestive. It is not satisfactorily explained by the theory that his subjects were brow-
beaten by Henry VIII. The second argument
which must be pondered is no less perplexing.
If the marriage difficulties of Henry VIII. were
simply and solely due to the sudden passion of the
king, then the sequence of events leading up to
the dissolution of the marriage are inexplicable.
Personal desires would not have led Henry to
complicated diplomatic scheming and frequent
requests to the Pope to deal with his case. On
the contrary, they would have led him to direct
action of a very different kind. It is easy to miss
the reasons why such action was impossible for
Henry, but to miss them is to lose one of the secrets
of the history of the period. Perhaps the most
damning evidence of Pope Clement's complete
failure to understand the English problem, a
failure that was to cost him so much, was revealed
in a letter showing that even as late as September
1530 the real issue was an enigma to him. In
that year Casale informed Henry VIII. that the
Pope had secretly proposed to him " that your
Majesty might be allowed two wives. I told him
I could not undertake to make any such proposition, because I did not know whether it would

satisfy your Majesty's conscience." The still small voice of Henry's conscience could, on occasion, wax most eloquent, and the reasons that provoked it will emerge more clearly when we have gone some way towards answering some of the questions already raised in this chapter.

The effort is worth making, for it will show how much deeper went the implications of the changes taking place than at first sight appears. Public sympathy sided with Catherine, but not unnaturally public opinion was ultimately directed towards the public interest, and public interest at this point of time was very intricately concerned with the marriage question in a way not altogether for Catherine's good. We have seen that much of the success of the work of Henry VII. followed the fact that he was the founder of a dynasty. What he built was not in danger of being left incomplete, because there was a successor who would be able to continue his work. Since Henry VII.'s day much more had been done. Men were beginning to realize the advantages they derived from the new strong government of Henry VIII. and Wolsey, and it was with misgivings approaching near to fear that they scanned the horizon for the shadows that would presage Henry's death. Inevitable that event must be, and yet no preparations they could think of would make its coming other than disastrous. The marriage with Catherine had been a tragic failure. From 1510 until 1518 there had been repeated hopes of the birth of an heir, but on each occasion the joy bells, which were to herald its coming, had been turned

into death tolls, and with the exception of that
of the infant Mary—born in February 1516—
there was no new birthday to be celebrated within
the royal circle. Henry had no legitimate son
to whom he could bequeath the responsibilities
of his kingdom. In the eyes of the world this
succession problem transcended in importance all
others. Without the hope of a dynasty there
could be no really permanent peace. The future
held the promise of anarchy and civil war such
as had been familiar in Lancastrian and Yorkist
days. Little wonder that men were awed at the
prospect. In such circumstances their hearts might
beat in sympathy with Catherine, but their heads
were filled with troubled thoughts about the
meaning of this unsatisfactory marriage. They
had little sympathy for Anne Boleyn, but they
could not view with equanimity the prospects
offered by the Spanish marriage which had failed
to provide an heir to the throne.

There is no need to explain at length the views
of Henry VIII. on this question of the succession,
but it will be realized that the sweeping general-
ization to the effect that there would have been
a divorce problem even if there had been no Anne
Boleyn is not without a grain of truth. Even
before that lady had begun to influence the king
his mind had been reflecting on the curious
fatality which seemed to haunt the births of all
his children. These reflections turned primarily
on considerations of state, and since such considerations dominated all marriage policy in the
case of royal personages during the sixteenth

127

century, so they were bound to play a large part in shaping the divorce policy of Henry VIII. The marriage with Anne Boleyn was no romantic adventure of a hot-headed youth. It had its unlovely moments when passion took control of the king's will, but it had its moments, too, when motives of political expediency held sway, and in these considered motives of policy lies much which clears the tortuous marriage question of its mystery. Henry's actions were dominated by the question of the succession. His desperate efforts to win papal consent to the annulment of his first marriage, and—when that failed—his grim determination to decorate his second marriage with all the trappings of legality, reveal his aims. If the Pope could not be made to declare the first marriage illegal, then an English archbishop must be given authority to do it in his place. The second marriage could not be of any use unless it held the promise of legitimate issue. For this cause it must at all costs bear such sanctions of legality as could be read into Cranmer's declaration of May 23, 1533, to the effect that Henry and Catherine had never been legally married. If canon law would not accept such an issue, then so much the worse for canon law. For the desolating truth which paralysed all compromise and brushed aside all sacrifices to expediency was this : the problem of the succession would not be solved by adding to it thorny problems of legitimacy. Due stress upon the question of the succession will explain much that otherwise is puzzling in Reformation history. It

makes clear the doubts tearing men's minds away
from Catherine's cause, and it makes more intelligible the peculiarly legal nature of the policy
which brought about the Reformation.

The popular view of Henry VIII. as a puppet
moved by nothing save his sensual desires hides
from view an all-important truth. He was in
reality the victim of a highly developed conscience.
Before the Reformation he spent much time in
cultivating it, and after that movement had begun
its course he spent equally as long in strangling it.
He succeeded on both occasions. His whole reign
is a tragedy of conscience more perfect than any
of the models Elizabethan poets were later to
conceive. The subject is one on which it is easy
to make cheap flippancies, but only a serious
recognition of the deep influence of the king's
conscience will take us to the roots of the problems
of the age. Henry was a theologian of no mean
ability. He was far too wise a man to waste
overmuch time in weaving into theories his firm
belief that God was personally intervening in the
fortunes of his house ; but his caution did not
make his firm belief in such divine attentions any
less pronounced. Naturally, therefore, he looked
upon his childless marriage as a comment made
by God, and before Anne Boleyn had awakened
the king's interest, contemplation on the divine
wrath had stirred to life the king's conscience.
There is, of course, nothing easier than cynicism.
The criticism which speaks of the royal conscience
as a plant of tender growth, peculiarly susceptible
to the fertilizing influences of expediency, would

simplify the task before us very considerably if it succeeded in disposing of Henry's troublesome voice satisfactorily : but it does not do so. The fact remains that whether we altogether believe in the ingenuous eloquence of the king's conscience or not, Henry told the world a great deal about it, and the complex issues that he thought—or said he thought—his conscience raised, were the issues which had to be faced in the real politics of his day.

Thus a succession question and a tender conscience combined with the alleged attractions of Anne Boleyn to call forth the project of a new marriage. It was a curious combination, fraught with strange results, for the English Reformation might not have been a unique phenomenon if these peculiar factors had not had a place in its creation. For good or evil they were there : but behind them loomed more powerful forces. They, too, had their place, and what that place was must be understood by any one who seeks an answer to the questions how and why an English parliament could make a royal excommunicate the Pope of England.

The vital link between the fortunes of the Church of Rome and the second marriage of Henry VIII. will be found in the diplomatic jugglery to which the interaction of the one upon the other gave rise. In asking for a reconsideration of his marriage, Henry knew that he was not asking for an unreasonable favour. Enough has been said already to show how marriage questions —be they royal marriages or those of ordinary men

and women—came under the special control of the
Church, and in taking the question to the Pope
for decision Henry was really acting as a most
orthodox Catholic. Moreover, there were special
considerations affecting this case. Everything
rested on a papal dispensation granted for the first
marriage—that of Henry to Catherine, the widow
of his brother. Henry might well argue that
what one Pope had given a successor might review,
though whether the papal view of the ease with
which the actions of a predecessor might be
brought into question would agree with Henry's
was a point which brought a pause into the
argument Henry was developing. When it is
remembered that others, even among Henry's
contemporaries, had received annulments of marriage in cases which were, at any rate, no more
deserving of consideration than that of Henry, it
will be understood that he had some cause for
being confident of success.

His calculations missed a forceful argument that
came from deeds accomplished. Wolsey's foreign
policy may dazzle by its brilliant cleverness ; but
it had failed because it was too clever, and the
most significant result of his work was that it
placed the Pope—who was to be the king's judge
—in the hands of Charles V. at a time when Henry
needed him. With Charles in control it needed
no great political insight to prophesy the result of
an inquiry into the marriage. Naturally Henry
sought to get the case heard in his own country,
and quite as naturally the Pope resisted the
inevitable result of an inquiry held under such

conditions. Now the moral is to be found in the
diplomacy which centred around this situation.
The divorce revealed, as hardly anything else
could have done, the state to which the Papacy
had sunk. Papal policy had made the head of the
Church Universal nothing better than an Italian
prince who schemed wars, and fought, and was
taken prisoner, just as any ordinary prince of this
world. He could be bargained with, tricked, and
in the last resort defied, just as any diplomatist
would have been in such an age. If we criticize
Henry for his policy towards Rome, we should
also bear in mind the provocation. The cynical
disregard of his high office, for which the Pope
was notorious, had as great bearing on the English
Reformation as had Henry's own desires.

What has been said so far has been by way of
illustration of the complications in the purely
personal problem of the divorce. It does not
solve the question before us, for if we seek the full
significance of those events our glance must take
in more than these few questions. Through all
the changing scenes since 1485 had run one logical
idea, to the working out of which the energies of
Henry VII. and Wolsey had been freely given.
Wide as were the issues the task involved, they
can be packed together into one short phrase.
From 1485 until 1530 sovereignty in England was
fighting feudal privilege wherever the two met.
Military metaphors do not adequately describe
what was taking place. Let us try another
analogy. The student of Tudor economic history
must have before his eyes a map of England

marked with open fields and strips, and indications
of the enclosures which were the beginning of the
end of mediæval economic organization.   The
student of Tudor constitutional history will find
it just as well worth while to make and use a map.
Upon it he will mark for mediæval times the strips
over which feudal privileges and franchises were
exercised.   But for Tudor times the maze of strips
will appear less complex.   The overmighty subject, ready to abuse his remnants of feudal privilege by using them in order to impede the course
of the law, obsolete franchises, the preponderating
influence of a daily weakening feudal class, these
can be gradually erased from the map.   In Tudor
constitutional history an enclosure movement was
in progress.   By fair means and by foul, by
stealthy encroachment, lapse of years, lucky accident and cunning, the owners of such strips of
privilege were being displaced.   There still remained, however, tracts of territory to be won
before consolidation would be complete.   Within
the state the most obstructive of all rivals to central
authority still lived on.   The very nature of the
Church as a corporation, the one permanent institution in a world of transitory things, made it a
deadly foe.   What it had it held for ever.   As
long as the Church possessed privileges, whose
position on the map is best indicated by awkward,
straggling strips of jurisdictional immunities
sprawled all over the land, there could be no
central authority with unrivalled powers.   The
national king could not come into his own while
an international Church shared with him authority

in those matters of worldly business which have
been suggested in an earlier chapter. Such a
conclusion was evident to every serious statesman
of the period. It was borne in upon the king's
mind with overpowering force when his own
personal affairs brought him face to face with
papal power. There could be one, and only one,
solution for a king who aimed at keeping all his
heritage and taking kingship yet a little farther on
the road towards absolute supremacy. The strips
of privilege still remaining with the Church must
be acquired by the sovereign. The ecclesiastical
legislation of the years 1526 to 1536 consists of a
number of enclosure acts, which ended for ever
the reservations of feudal privilege belonging to
the Church in England.

To this end Wolsey's rule had surely pointed
the way. As we have seen, in that one man had
been combined the all-important elements of
sovereignty. They were symbolized whenever he
took a walk. " There was also borne before him,"
Cavendish said, " the Great Seal of England, and
then his Cardinal's hat." He was on the verge of
the solution of an age-old problem. He was the
representative of God and Cæsar. Is it to be
wondered at that Henry VIII. saw the advantages
in the days when his projects were not going well?
Was there not logic behind a king who would also
be pope? In the Reformation there were mighty
issues, but the greatest of them was not the
question of a royal marriage. A king of England
was striving to add the one thing needful if he was
to be really king. By becoming supreme head of

the Church, Henry was striving to get control of the privileges, jurisdictions, and authority without which no king could be supreme in his own country.

Such thoughts should suggest the reasons behind Henry's actions, but there is another problem to be solved. Obviously the prize which Henry sought was one which justified his efforts, but no study of the period will go far without revealing that behind the king there was another and a greater power. It is possible to hold strong opinions about what happened. It is probable that they will lead to a condemnation of Henry's enclosure of ecclesiastical privileges as severe as that passed on many a Tudor upstart who sneaked land from his weaker neighbours. It must, however, be remembered that Henry enclosed by act of parliament. We may say that Henry's policy destroyed canon law, but we must at the same time remember that it made English statute law. We may even go so far as to say that it was the policy of one man, and that that man acted under motives of a personal and most questionable kind. All this may be perfectly true. What is equally true is that the policy of one man was endorsed by a parliament of respectable Englishmen, and if any one is to be blamed for what occurred, Henry can only be regarded as the scapegoat for a nation. How came this acquiescence in Henry's policy?

The facile theory which explains it all by the argument that parliament was packed in the royal interests, and was only the mouthpiece for the royal will, would be admirable if it could be conclusively proved. Unfortunately that is no easier than it would be to offer complete evidence in an opposite direction. The well-known instance sometimes used to prove the use of royal influence—a letter written from Ralph Sadler to Cromwell concerning an election to the parliament of 1529—is what it has been called, " singularly inconclusive." Even if proved, it would only be one instance, and it seems impossible to collect sufficient examples to justify any dogmatic assertions. On the other hand, the attitude of Henry's parliaments was not such as suggests complete subservience to royal policy, and the explanation of the legislation of those sessions must be sought elsewhere than in the simple accusation of royal interference.

Some part of such an explanation will be found not in the parliament but in the Church. It cannot be doubted that the facility with which Henry obtained legislative sanction for his measures against the Church was due as much to the anxiety of his subjects to see the policy of royal consolidation carried out as it was to Henry's own desire for supremacy in England. And the explanation of that feeling on the part of his subjects is two-edged. It lies first and foremost in the certainty that many Englishmen regarded the feudal privileges of the Church as an anachronism; and, secondly, in the conviction shared by many that there were definite benefits to be gained from the strengthening of the royal power. The Church itself supplied the reason for the first belief ; the success of Henry's rule supplied the reason for the second. For the failure of the Church to use its privileges in the interests of the community had bred discontent at its continued possession of its privileges, and the fate of Wolsey enabled Henry to retain the advantages of his strong rule without incurring the unpopularity that rule had aroused.

Long before the Reformation Parliament met there had been a scandalous case which had roused anti-clerical feeling to a high pitch. In 1514 a London merchant, named Richard Hunne, was imprisoned on a charge of heresy. There was probably something in the charge, but Hunne's immediate trouble was due to a dispute with a priest who claimed a bearing sheet as a mortuary fee for the burial of a child. The dispute was less interesting than the sequel. The imprisoned man was found hanging dead in his cell. A jury, not satisfied by the theory of suicide, accused the bishop of London's chancellor and his servants of murder. There was a great scandal, and feeling ran high against the clergy. Hunne's case was a straw showing the way of the wind, and it led indirectly to a more important issue. In 1515 the abbot of Winchcombe preached a topical sermon at Paul's, in which he defended benefit of clergy. As a result of protests, Henry arranged a disputation on the subject, and in the arguments of Dr. Standish and others he learned what advanced thinkers thought of Church privileges and the power of the king. His own speeches at the time, and his actions later, showed that he was an apt pupil, and that in his keeping the rights of kingship were not likely to be annexed by an aggressive Church.

The interest of such incidents lies in the signs they reveal of a bitter anti-ecclesiastical spirit growing up in the country, and a glance at the legislation of the Reformation Parliament is enough to indicate the influence of such ideas upon events. The long series of acts was ushered in by some which dealt specifically with abuses in the Church in England. It was not without cause that the work of parliament ran on well-defined lines. Popular enthusiasm was stimulated by attacks on the Church which had as their aim the removal of such abuses. It was only after such legislation had been accomplished that parliament went on to consider the acts which were to cut the English Church away from Rome ; and it was only after that work was well on the way to completion that the statutes embodying the more constructive changes were evolved. There was clever statesmanship behind the order of events. Parliament was skilfully handled in the sense that its peculiar grievances against the Church formed the starting-point for legislation. The manipulation was, however, a signal comment on the state of opinion about the Church. Henry benefited by the hostility that institution had aroused against itself through its failure to achieve its ideals, but that hostility was something for which Henry himself could not have been responsible. If men were attacking ecclesiastical abuses, they were doing so not for any special love they bore Anne Boleyn— not, indeed, for any special enthusiasm Henry him-

self attracted : they were attacking those features
in its organization which they looked upon as a
menace to the community. They were hostile to
those of the clergy who were busied over payment
of tithe of mint and anise and cummin, and
oblivious to the weightier matters of the law—
judgment, mercy, and faith. It is a point of some
significance that the first attack upon the Church in
England centred on fees for burials and administration of wills. The attack was not the first nor
the last great constitutional issue in English history
to begin with a grievance affecting the pockets of
Englishmen. With regard to what followed—the
attacks on benefit of clergy and sanctuary—
enough has already been said to justify that feeling
of uneasiness with which Englishmen viewed these
ecclesiastical privileges. They provided a sufficient nucleus of grievances to cause grave dis-
affection ; and they are sufficient proof of the fact
—never to be forgotten in the history of the breach
with Rome—that the political considerations pre-
dominant in all the questions of the time, from
that of the divorce to the events leading to the fall
of Cromwell, were the direct motive force of the
early attack.

If one of two errors had to be made in estimating
the factors behind the English Reformation, it
would probably be less serious to forget altogether
what is generally called Lutheran influence in
England before 1529, than to make special emphasis upon it as an important factor in later
events. By Lutheranism may be implied more
than is usually meant by the continental use of that

word. For our purposes it may be taken to indicate all those anti-papal forces which criticized indulgences, saint worship, superstitious practices, the mass, and which had as an ideal greater insistence on the knowledge of Scripture as the basis of faith and worship. In this sense of the word there were clearly Lutherans in England before the Reformation, and not all of them were in touch with continental thought. Hidden springs of Lollardy still formed oases in English religious life. The available evidence of heresy cases before 1529 is not numerically great, but it is sufficient to show that heretical beliefs were disseminated, and there can be little doubt that the political movement gained momentum from such prevailing ideas. At the same time, when due allowance has been made for the influence of such ideas, the Reformation must remain for us pre-eminently political in quality throughout the reign of Henry VIII. An element of doctrinal change was introduced, but it must be carefully considered, and no hasty generalizations should be made about the nature of the breach with Rome when viewed on its doctrinal side.

It was not that Henry VIII. was incapable of embarking on such controversial innovations. Theology was an early enthusiasm of his which he never neglected, nor was he without very definite ideas on the theological questions of his age. His opinions, however, remained orthodox almost consistently throughout his reign, and there is small reason to suppose that he was at any time anxious to carry out sweeping changes in the doctrinal

life of the Church similar to those he was developing in its organization. His active interest in theology had been stirred to the depths by the appearance of Luther, with whose teaching he had no
patience, and in the early part of 1521 he was
studying the works of that reformer with a view
to contradicting their ideas. Reading confirmed
his opinions. By May 1521 St. Paul's Church-
yard was being used for a public incineration of
Luther's books, at which Fisher preached to a
congregation which included Wolsey, the archbishop of Canterbury, the bishop of London, the
papal nuncio, and other distinguished men. By
September a beautifully bound copy of the king's
own book—the *Assertio Septem Sacramentorum*—
had been duly presented to Pope Leo. In return-
ing thanks for the gift, Leo spoke with enthusiasm
of a king who could use his pen as well as he could
fight, and in October he followed his praises by a
title for Henry VIII. The future excommunicate
was to be known as the Defender of the Faith.
The book has no outstanding qualities that would
suggest it as the work of a genius, and there seems
no reason why Henry should not have whatever
credit the book merits as his own unaided work.
Much was to happen by 1536, but on the whole
Henry did not modify his opinions on the general
doctrinal controversies of the period, and to the
end of his reign he was no follower of Luther.

All the same, some declaration of faith there had
to be. It was impossible to revolutionize the organization of the English Church without causing
considerable interference with its teachings and its

creeds. An attempt to meet the new needs was made in 1536 in the Ten Articles, written by Henry, edited by Cranmer, and accepted by the Convocation of the Clergy. They were not revolutionary. The three sacraments of baptism, penance, and the Eucharist were retained, and images in churches, invocations to saints, and Catholic ceremonies were still allowed, though qualifications as to their efficacy for the remission of sins were added. But there were traces of change. The Bible and the Three Creeds were to be the essentials of orthodoxy, and the repudiation of indulgences, the manner of justification, and the assertion of a Real Presence were the outstanding features in the statement. On the whole, it may be said that the Ten Articles were a compromise between old thought and new, and the objective of those who drafted them was quite clearly the establishment of a state of peace within the English Church after recent changes, rather than an attempt to introduce the continental Reformation.

It could hardly be hoped that a solution to the problems the Reformation raised could be so easily reached. From 1536 until the death of Henry in 1547 they still remained unsettled, and in these later years what was old and new in religious thought were struggling for supremacy in England. On the whole, victory went to the old. Conservative forces were sufficiently strong to make any movement towards advanced doctrinal reform too dangerous, even had Henry VIII. himself been disposed to encourage such a movement. Thus all the later schemes are conservative, and aim at a compromise with radical reform. The Bishops' Book of 1537 goes back to the old, the Injunctions of 1536 and 1538 are primarily concerned with matters of administration, and cannot be said to introduce revolutionary ideas, while the notorious statute of Six Articles of 1539—" the whip with six strings," as it was called, because of the penalties attached to each article—was decidedly meant as a deterrent from further change. Its articles definitely affirmed the doctrine of transubstantiation, justified communion in one kind, enforced celibacy and the keeping of monastic vows upon the clergy, authorized as necessary the continuation of private masses and auricular confession. These were to be enforced by the pains and penalties of burning and forfeiture of goods. Such articles succeeded in the work for which they were made. They frightened the leaders of advanced thought, and steadied the doctrinal drift. For the religion they recognized was in essence the old Catholic faith. There would never more be a Roman Pope with any permanent authority in England, but the foundations on which the Roman Church was built were the model for the doctrine of the Church whose head was the king of England.

Henry's cautious policy did not mean that sweeping changes were not taking place. Extreme opinions filtered into England from the continent, and the king's own policy was deliberately designed to stimulate, within limits, the reaction away from Rome. It was to this end that scripture study was encouraged. The more men knew their bibles the less tolerant they would become of papal claims, and it was in Henry's interest to foster such ideas. It is interesting to watch the drift towards new things. The translation of the New Testament made by Tyndale in 1526 had been hunted out of England by Wolsey and Henry because of its heresies ; but the call for something to take its place could not be ignored. As the years passed the substitute was shaped. Coverdale's translation of the Bible appeared in 1536, and was licensed by the king in 1537. It was not satisfactory. In the same year we find Cranmer recommending another version known as Matthew's Bible. Its interest comes from the sources from which it was compiled, for it was nothing more than a fusion of the works by Tyndale and Coverdale. An " improved " version known as the Great Bible appeared in 1539. In the next year this version appeared again with a preface by Cranmer, a fact which later gave it the name of Cranmer's Bible. And so the voice of Tyndale was heard again in the land! This insistence on bible reading, and the wide dissemination of the scriptures which is found reflected in the Injunctions, indicates royal policy and explains the continued drift towards reform thought which led to the struggles for supremacy between old and new in the later years of the reign.

In Cranmer, whose views on the divorce had shown Henry his value, and had raised him—very much against his will—to be archbishop of Canterbury in March 1533, Henry had a guide who had no uncertain faith in the good that the State could do for the reform of an impure Church. The full implications of this idea he had hardly realized in Henry's reign. In touch with German thought as he was, Cranmer could not be without opinions upon questions of doctrinal reform, but he was not a Lutheran. In Henry's reign he saw that it was not as yet wise to go very far along the road of change. He knew that the time would come for further advance, but the intervening years he spent in the study of doctrine and liturgies. His time was to come after Henry was dead, and the harvest of the quiet years he was allowed to spend in study during Henry's reign was to be reaped under Edward VI. What influence he had—and with Henry VIII. it was great—was in the direction of slow reform ; but his real work was to be done in the future.

For the future, too, remained the question of doctrinal reformation. The years with which we have been dealing were years filled with great events, but politics was the recurring theme in all of them. The breach with Rome had been the work of men whose real interest was the State. The deeds and not the creeds of papal Rome account for its disfavour in the eyes of those who had control of English policy during the reign of Henry VIII. They happened upon problems bigger than they knew, and those they could not solve they handed on to their successors.

CHAPTER VII

MOST of the changes of Henry VIII.'s reign which had such momentous effects upon England had been brought near to completion by about 1537. There remained ten years during which Henry was to govern his people in all the majesty of his newly-acquired powers. Those ten years were unlovely years, during which the evil features of the reign came fully into prominence, and if it were not for the fact that those very evils provide an indispensable commentary upon the implications of the new sovereignty in State and Church, it would be pleasant to pass them by without comment.

The change which took place in the person of the king himself during those years is symbolic of a subtle but definite degeneration which seemed to come over the whole of his realm. It is a change for the worse, which cannot pass unnoticed by those familiar with the impression Henry had made upon contemporaries in his youth. In 1519 a Venetian living in England painted an attractive pen-portrait of the young king. " And first of all," he says, " his Majesty is twenty-nine years old, and extremely handsome ; nature could not have

146

done more for him ; he is much handsomer than any other sovereign in Christendom, a great deal handsomer than the King of France ; very fair, and his whole frame admirably proportioned. On learning that Francis I. wore a beard, he allowed his own to grow, and as it is reddish, he has now got a beard which looks like gold. He is very accomplished : a good musician : composes well : is a most capital horseman : a fine jouster : speaks good French, Latin, and Spanish : is very religious : hears three masses daily when he hunts, and sometimes five on other days : he hears the *office* every day in the Queen's chamber—that is to say, vespers and compline. He is very fond of hunting, and never takes this diversion without tiring eight or ten horses, which he causes to be stationed beforehand along the line of country he may mean to take ; and when one is tired he mounts another, and before he gets home they are all exhausted. He is extremely fond of tennis, at which game it is the prettiest thing in the world to see him play, his fair skin glowing through a shirt of the finest texture."

It is a picture which could be matched by others from those early years when Henry had attracted the attention of foreign visitors and gained the affection of the best type of his subjects, to whom he appeared as the flower of English manhood. But after 1537 the charm was lost. Self-indulgence, the cares of state, and the anxieties of the later years had coarsened the mind, soured the temper, and robbed the king of his better nature. Power corrupts, and the desolating influence of despotic power made havoc of Henry's character. His physical attractions had also gone. The young athlete had degenerated into a bloated, unwieldy figure, suffering agonies from a diseased leg, and finding movement so difficult that mechanical devices had to be used to move him from room to room. A later extant portrait tells the tale, and the unfavourable impression of Henry which is popularly current is based largely on the fact that the Henry of this picture is better known than the Henry of the opening of the reign. It is wrong to judge him and his reign from such an impression. It should not be forgotten that Henry was only fifty-five years and seven months old when he died, that for the better part of his reign the impression given in the earlier years is a fairer view of him than that of the later period, and that until after the divorce, at any rate, he compares favourably in matters of morality with other sixteenth century kings. Such reflections do not by any means erase the stains upon the last years of Henry's reign. They ought to mitigate our judgment of him, but they can never dispel the gloom which hovers over the period with which this chapter is mainly concerned.

Nor does the problem of the succession and the royal marriage, which continues to haunt these years, help to lighten the gloom. That question, responsible as it was for the storm of the earlier years, was not settled by the marriage of Henry to Anne Boleyn. On the contrary, around it there seemed to gather all the misfortune of Henry's life, and the wearisome story of the king's attempts to

solve it ran on through the greater part of the last
decade with horrible results. The pathos is of a
peculiar quality. The events connected with the
question do not make high tragedy, for an element
of the ridiculous runs through the drama, and it
has a disconcerting effect upon our impression of a
king who sought at all times and in all circumstances to convey an impression of his regality to
those with whom he came in contact. On the
other hand, the question cannot be lightly dismissed, for it does form a tragedy of sorts :
the shadow of death broods for ever on the stage.
As early as May 19, 1536, Anne Boleyn's hour of
triumph was spent. The king's disillusionment,
Anne's follies, and the old problem—that of the
succession—had combined to work their worst,
and the woman whose history must be for ever
interwoven with the destinies of her country had
ended her meteoric career at the hands of the
executioner. The day after her death Henry
married Jane Seymour, and the birth of her son—
the future Edward VI.—on October 12, 1537,
seemed at last to have solved the greatest of
Henry's difficulties. Twelve days later Jane Seymour was dead. For over two years Henry remained a widower. Then the machinations of
Cromwell, the necessities of foreign policy, the
king's personal wishes—all combined to bring into
English politics the Princess Anne of Cleves.
Henry, *malgré lui*, married her on July 6, 1540, but
the rude nickname he coined for her when first he
met her—the Flanders mare—is a sufficient indication of his ideas on Cromwell's choice. The

comedy of this weird marriage, in which Henry was content to do what his adviser told him to do, was only transitory. Tragedy was not far away, and although Anne escaped with the happy release of a declaration of nullity of marriage made by convocation, a greater than she was cast for the tragic part. As will be seen later, this marriage meant the end of Cromwell's schemes. Anne was indeed fortunate. She lived in affluence at the royal expense until 1558, with all the advantages and none of the disadvantages of being Henry's wife. In July 1540 Catherine Howard caught the royal eye, and became queen. She was dead, executed for the sins of her youth, by February 1542. In July 1543 Catherine Parr was married to the king. She was the last woman whose name was to be linked to that of Henry. There is little to be said of her save the redeeming fact that she brings at any rate a suggestion of respectability into Henry's matrimonial affairs.

This melancholy story of Henry's marriages would not be worth telling at greater length. Its only interest lies in the way it illustrates the gruesome element that crept into the later years of the reign. Tragedy ruled the scene, and many bloodstains soil the pattern being woven in those years. The reckoning of death is too lengthy to be narrated in full, but the procession of ghosts walking unavenged is awe-inspiring. In 1534 a poor demented creature, Elizabeth Barton, went to her doom, dragging with her friars and monks, because she published prophecies against the king's life. Greater names—those of More and

Fisher—followed. There was the group that perished with Anne Boleyn ; the cruelty displayed in trampling underfoot the Pilgrimage of Grace ; the vengeance wreaked upon the Pole family in 1538; the fall and death of Cromwell in 1540; the attack upon the Howards, with the trial and death of the younger, Surrey, in 1547. These are only instances of a list easily made longer, but they are enough to indicate the horrors linked up with Henry's rise to mastery. Supremacy was bought at a price.

It would be a depressing—and futile—task to give the narrative of the later years as a series of murders, judicial and otherwise. A much more profitable study can be undertaken. For below the surface were the deeper problems which have to be analysed before the contribution made by this period to the general development of our history can be appreciated. By 1537 Henry had reached the pinnacle of his power. Supremacy had been achieved, but that was not the end. There remained the solution of the difficulties to which supremacy gave rise.

The first of those problems leads back to the years already surveyed, for if the interest of Thomas Cromwell's career lies in the years after the end of the Reformation Parliament, it should be remembered that he had been active in the work done while that parliament was in session. In him is to be found the inspiration of much of the policy whereby Henry achieved his ends. In him, too, is to be read the awful moral of supremacy achieved, and a study of his work

sheds light on Tudor history at a crucial point.
Like other prominent statesmen of the time, he
was the product of the new system—a new man,
born into the family of a blacksmith at Putney,
and educated by journeyings to and fro in the
world. His university had been Europe as well
as England, and his wide range of qualifications
had been gained in many spheres. He had been
a soldier of fortune, an estate agent, moneylender,
wool merchant, and solicitor; and his travels
had taken him to Flanders and Italy. He had
touched on the fringes, at any rate, of the " new
learning," and during his journeyings in Italy
the theories of Machiavelli had been brought to
his notice. Even in the years when he was attach-
ing himself to the retinue of Wolsey—somewhere
between 1513 and 1520—he is supposed to have
advised Pole to read that author's *Il Principe*, and
his own career was deliberately dedicated to the
ideal of the absolute monarchy sketched in the
Italian's book. There are those who deny that
Machiavelli's works were known to Cromwell,
but they cannot as yet be said to have proved their
contention. In any case, even though their view
be accepted, it still remains true that the new
spirit of statecraft—for which the name of Machiavelli is the symbol—was wholly in keeping with
that which animated Cromwell's policy. Methods
as well as objectives were learned. In Thomas
Cromwell all the unscrupulous cunning, the
unswerving course towards a well-defined end,
the realist conception of politics characteristic
of the Italian statecraft of the day, found their way

into English public life. His own career illustrates Cromwell's skill in the art of self-advancement. In 1523 he had succeeded in entering parliament. He owed his first steps towards advancement to the help of Wolsey, whom he sedulously cultivated in the days of the cardinal's greatness, yet he succeeded in surviving the fate of his master without making his desertion of his benefactor too obvious. By 1530 he had evidently entered the service of the king. By 1533 the foreigner Chapuys knew him for the power behind the throne, though it is evident that his ascendancy had begun before that date. Throughout the years from 1533 until 1540 Cromwell's fortunes stood high. None of the momentous decisions which led to the policy of these years was taken without his knowledge, many of the plans put into operation were his own invention, some were his own work. All were centred upon one objective. From beginning to end of his career his mind was fixed on plans to make his king supreme in England, and himself the indispensable minister of his king. All he cared for was the growth of the royal supremacy and the possibilities of self-advancement such growth implied. He brought into the politics of his day a sinister word that was the symbol of his own business career and the token of the new age opening out before the rising middle class of England. For with Thomas Cromwell money became the keynote of policy, and all the evil influences inseparably connected with that word became the dominant motives of statecraft. At a time when Henry VIII. was beginning to realize that success in the attainment of his aims was impossible without increased financial resources— at a time, indeed, when Henry's debts were more than embarrassing—Cromwell whispered into his ear the fateful secret that was to bring out the most sordid features of Reformation history, make Henry victorious in the struggle with the Church, and raise Cromwell to high place. It was the nemesis of his scheming that success ultimately rendered him superfluous in the State, and it would have been well for him if he had taken more thoroughly to heart a lesson the Italian master had taught. For Machiavelli discovered that a general principle governed politics—one that never, or rarely, fails—and that " he who is the cause of another becoming powerful is ruined : because that predominancy has been brought about either by astuteness or else by force, and both are distrusted by him who has been raised to power." Cromwell's subsequent history was to show the truth of that deduction, but that time had not come as early as 1533. His sesame to Henry's heart was to find for him a ready hearing. It was a counsel of spoliation. Cromwell was the soul of the activities which culminated in the dissolution of the monasteries.

In ascribing the initiation of such a policy to Thomas Cromwell, it must be emphasized that there was nothing new in the scheme, and Cromwell was not the first to yield to the temptation that came as a result of glancing at the wealth of the Church. The first suggestion of the secularization of Church property came early in English history, but it was made under very special circumstances. The alien priories in England had, at an early date, been looked upon with suspicion because they owed allegiance to monastic foundations abroad. John had taken the opportunity of despoiling them of their revenues, and in 1285 Edward I. had followed his example. In 1337 Edward III. had acted on these precedents, and in 1414 all alien priories in England had been taken into the king's hands. The fifteenth century held indications that the monastic system as a whole was being looked upon with suspicion. It would appear that the Lollards in 1410 had even gone so far as to suggest that the lands of bishops and greater abbots should be secularized, and the suggestion had been strengthened by the argument that this would provide subsistence for earls and knights for the defence of the king, while it would also leave £20,000 for the king's use. The suggestion did not come to anything in practical politics, but it is an interesting forecast of later policy. Even more suggestive, however, was the criticism implied in the foundation of colleges and hospitals, which became a marked feature of the fifteenth century. Men were turning from monasticism, and were finding an outlet for their good works in schemes for charity and education of a different kind. The work of Lady Margaret, mother of Henry VII., in the foundation of professorships at Oxford and Cambridge, was a sign of the times, and it was a prelude to Wolsey's plans. Thus the new policy was only a fulfilment of earlier ideas, and Cromwell's claim to credit—or infamy—lies not in the novelty of his ideas, but in the thoroughness with which he copied the ideas of Wolsey. The scheme, fertile in far-reaching results, and destined to be the source of more fierce controversy than probably any other event by which the breach with Rome was achieved, can be set down in few words. In 1535 Thomas Cromwell—layman as he was—became vicar-general, with power to exercise all the jurisdictional and ecclesiastical functions which had fallen to the king as the supreme head of the Church, and with licence to visit, or appoint deputies to visit, all religious houses. Between October 1535 and February 1536 he and his servants were busy collecting evidence of the condition of the monasteries. The results of their investigations were embodied in reports, and finally an act was passed which stated that all religious houses with an income of less than £200 a year were given to the king, in order that their possessions " should be used and converted to better uses." There was very skilful policy behind this act. It would be hard to make out that there was much difference between the standards of morality in the smaller and the greater monasteries ; but Henry and Cromwell were making the first move in a deep scheme. In order to gain their ends they sought to win over the abbots of the greater monasteries to consent to the dissolution of the smaller houses in the hope that this gesture would save their own foundations. No house divided against itself can stand. It was to be the turn of the greater monasteries as soon as the fate of the smaller houses had been decided. By further visitations and by threats other houses were persuaded to surrender voluntarily, and by 1539 another act extended the spoliation to the greater monasteries. By the first act the property of 376 religious houses had fallen to the crown. By the second, the surrender of 200 greater houses and 200 priories was legalized. In those years there were enacted all over England scenes such as that at Canterbury, where the riches of the tomb of St. Thomas were taken away in twenty-six cartloads, to be used as the royal pleasure should dictate. How great the spoils it is difficult to estimate, for more was at stake than jewels ; and in making calculations rents, leases, royalties, tithes, buildings, have also to be taken into account. The value of these is naturally very difficult to ascertain.

Like all other aspects of Henry's Reformation policy, the dissolution of the monasteries had about it a veneer of legality which makes it possible to advance a superficial argument in favour of his policy. Justice and legality must not, however, be confused. They were never synonymous terms in the mind of Henry VIII. None would deny that the monasteries had declined in utility in the late fifteenth century, and that grave faults could be found with them, even although the findings of prejudiced commissioners sent out by Cromwell with a brief in favour of dissolution be not accepted as reliable evidence of wholesale

corruption.   The religious houses, like the Church
in general, were passing through a period of
secularization, and it is not difficult to uncover
many instances of evils prevalent in monastic
organization.   The common charges against the
monks vary from drunkenness to absence from
religious services, from brawls, murders, gross
immorality to accusations of extravagance, love
of luxury, worldliness.   A good case can be made
for the statement that many houses were in a state
of decay, that their finances were in disorder,
that their discipline had become so lax that it was
practically non-existent.   All such accusations
carry with them a certain amount of truth which
may be easily substantiated from the records of
the time ; but the main argument of those who
make such accusations in support of the dissolution
is another and more vulnerable one.   All they say
about the evils of the system is intended to support
the principle that the end justifies the means.
And the damning answer to their argument is the
indisputable one that the end was never attained.
It is at least arguable that the dissolution of the
monasteries might have been justifiable if their
wealth had been " used and converted to better
uses," as the statute professed it was to be used.
If, for instance, it had been applied to the ends
Wolsey had in view when he initiated his policy :
the supply of an educational system in the interests of the " new learning " might have been
more beneficial to the community in general than
the retention of such wealth in the hands of a close
corporation of monks could ever hope to be.

But such a result was not attained. The wealth taken from the monasteries was used—it would appear that it was deliberately used—for purposes of a very different kind. It has been estimated that out of the proceeds of the property confiscated by the State, an amount equal to a yearly value of £90,000 was either given away for nothing or was sold—often at nominal prices—to a group of persons whose number did not reach much more than a thousand. Thus, under cover of a religious reformation a policy of indefensible robbery was carried out, and the dissolution of the monasteries was made the means of pandering to the selfish land hunger of a favoured few.

What, then, was the real significance of the policy ? It matters little for the moment whether we view the dissolution as a political move deserving of nothing but the severest condemnation, or whether we see in it a policy justifiable because it purged the Church of flagrant abuses. The real problem to which it gave rise is more important. For the policy of dissolution was yet another expression of the objects of the political reformation. It was a gesture whereby the dominant State overrode the Church. It was another blow at corporations over which the State had previously had no control. By challenging the Church on this point, Henry and Cromwell were working out the logical implications of the policy whereby the Church was reduced to subservience, and the sequestration of Church lands followed inevitably on the withdrawal of Church privileges. There were other results of some consequence. The dissolution of the monasteries put into the hands of the government a convenient means of binding together an important section of English society in support of its Reformation policy. The middle class, which benefited most by the transfer of the Church lands, was naturally to be found on the side whence they had gained advantages, and it is a cynical comment on the success of this policy and the cunning of its initiators that not even the reaction again towards Rome—when it came in Mary's day—was powerful enough to win their support for the restoration of Church lands. Nor was this all. The dissolution had a result that was not the less serious because it was probably unpremeditated. If the members of the House of Lords under Henry VII. be counted, it will be found that there were 49 spiritual peers and 29 temporal peers. After the dissolution the proportion of spiritual peers to temporal peers was as 21 is to some figure fluctuating between 36 and 50. Much has been said about the balance of power in the reign of Henry VIII. Here is the most significant of all shiftings of balance. The House of Lords, as a result of the dissolution, had a lay majority. How much that was to mean for the remainder of the Tudor period can only be realized when it is remembered that a large part of the legislative work of the years after Henry VIII., until the end of the Tudor period, continued to deal with ecclesiastical affairs. In the decision of religious matters a lay majority had the last word. When the cumulative influence of all these consequences of the policy of dissolution is brought to mind, it will be difficult to find any adjective other than Machiavellian to apply to the suggestions Thomas Cromwell had imparted to his royal master.

It was the policy initiated by the first Act of Dissolution that brought to a head the feelings hostile to the innovations of the Reformation. These demonstrations were the outward expression of grave dissatisfaction with the men who were forcing changes in the organization and doctrine of the Church, were despoiling the monasteries, and under pressure of government needs were increasing taxation. The first of them, in Lincoln-shire in 1536, was put down without great diffi-culty; but the Pilgrimage of Grace of 1536 was a more dangerous threat. Led by Robert Aske, a lawyer, the men of Yorkshire rose in protest against the attack on the monasteries, though deeper economic causes helped to strengthen their resistance, and their hatred of Cromwell was revealed by their anxiety to get him removed from the king's council. Aske, whose sincere desire for a peaceful reform of grievances led him to place too great a faith in negotiation, lost his chance of action and played into Henry's hands. But the commons he was leading were not de-ceived by royal promises, and further trouble occurred at Hull and Scarborough. Even after the ruthless policy of repression that was enforced, another outburst occurred in Westmorland and Cumberland. None of the risings succeeded. Sovereignty was too firmly established, Cromwell was too strong, the potentialities of the antimonastic schemes were too profitable to be checked by those forces within the State whose love of the old roused them against the innovations of which this period was so full.

In these ways the problem raised by the claim of the State to be supreme, a problem which found expression in the sequestration of the revenues of corporations, was one which came to a head in this last phase of Henry's reign. It opened on to grave considerations, for it was a question symbolizing the political theory which regarded monarchy and its interests as the highest good of the State. Before the king nothing could stand. Wealth must be sacrificed, corporations were as nothing when they stood in the way of his advancement. The greed for land, which was stimulated rather than satisfied by the dissolution of the monasteries, is a subject for the moralist ; but to the student of English political life the attitude of the government towards the spoliation of the Church is an eloquent comment on the evolution of the monarchy and a sign of the emergence of the all-powerful State.

Other implications no less arresting in character mark these last years. They bring the reader face to face with the terrible logic of events. They find their fullest expression in the deaths of Fisher and More ; but these tragedies are only indicative of the new spirit which entered English politics after supremacy had been attained. Fisher and More were the victims in the conflict of old and new ideas. Fisher had made no secret of the side he championed. It was not that of the

king, and when the case of Elizabeth Barton came
into prominence in 1534 he was implicated.
More had refrained from taking an active part
in the politics of supremacy. As a lawyer he had
too profound a respect for acts of parliament to
gird against facts accomplished, but he too was
implicated. The position was a difficult one.
Here were two men who were rightly regarded
as leaders of public opinion. If they could not
be induced to support Henry, what hope had the
king of success ? They had to be forced to take
a side. For Fisher the future was black, for his
antagonism to Henry's divorce—an antagonism
not always tactfully displayed—marked him out
for reprisals. It is the case of More that is really
interesting. In March 1534 the Act of Succession
had been passed. It authorized the enforcement
of an oath of obedience, but the terms of the oath
were left to be drawn up by commissioners, and
the pledge they evolved was rigorous. In April
More was called before the council to take the
oath. It was a commitment he would not venture,
for it held three clauses he could not accept. It
declared the marriage with Anne valid, annulled
that of Catherine, and attacked the primacy of the
Pope. He was prepared to recognize the accomplished fact of Anne's marriage, but he would not
go further. This was not far enough for the king,
so both More and Fisher were sent to the Tower.
In November 1534 the Act of Supremacy was
passed. Fisher and More had been condemned
to perpetual imprisonment, but the matter could
not be allowed to rest there. The absence of

their support was too dangerous for the king. In April 1535 they were again asked for their opinions on the statutes, but their replies were unsatisfactory. And then the criminal folly of the head of the Roman Church destroyed all hope for Fisher. In May the Pope made him a cardinal. The thunder of the royal wrath followed. In June Fisher was tried, and by 22nd June he was dead. On July 1, 1535, More was tried before a special commission consisting of ten peers and ten judges, presided over by lord chancellor Audley. The indictment accused him of attempting to deprive the king of his title of Supreme Head of the Church. He was found guilty, and by 6th July he, too, had gone to execution.

The "simple ignoraunte woman and somwhat worldly too," who was a good, albeit a shrewish, wife to Thomas More, was puzzled that her husband could so play the fool as to lie in a close, filthy prison and be content to be shut up amongst mice and rats when he might be at liberty and in the favour of the king and council if he would take the oath, as all the bishops and best learned of the realm had done. Dame Alice was not the first to proclaim the advantages of expediency, but More would not have deserved the high place he occupies in the intellectual life of his age if he had been blind to the ultimate realities behind its political and religious difficulties. For him the future seemed to hold so much that was calamitous. The unity of Christendom was being broken before his eyes, the splendid promise of the renaissance was wilting under the hot blasts of sectarian controversies, the materialism that was the keynote of the new age was heaping up social and economic problems which seemed to be insoluble. Most ominous of all, there rose before him the Moloch of triumphant monarchy. It was difficult for men to dogmatize about the new statecraft since it implied so much that was good mixed with so much that was evil. For lack of a standard of values they might be excused when they succumbed to the suggestions of expediency. For More, however, there was no such easy way. He had found a principle whereby to take the measure of this new theory and practice of politics. It was one for which death itself was not too great a price. It went to the root of the matter. More would have been prepared to say that an act of parliament could turn a man into a king ; he could not admit that it could make a man a Pope. " Suppose that the Parliament would make a lawe that God shoulde not be God, woulde you then, Maister Riche, saye that God were not God ? Noe, Sir, quothe he, that I would not : sith noe Parliament maye make any suche lawe. Noe more, sayd Sir Thomas More, . . . coulde the Parliament make the Kinge Supreme Heade of the Churche." The whole problem lies there. The omnicompetent State was facing its first challenge. If More were victorious all was lost. Supremacy could mean nothing less than supremacy. The most attractive Englishman of the sixteenth century had to be sacrificed for the glory of the new-born State.

Thomas Cromwell had played his part in forcing

that issue, but neither he nor any other Tudor statesman could solve it. The deaths of Fisher and More were tragedies that ushered in the new monarchy, and although they took place in the years prior to that last decade of the reign which we are discussing in this chapter, they must be studied in connection with those years, because they are the first and clearest illustration of the problems before the new sovereignty.

Cromwell's chief assistance to Henry VIII. was to be the building up of the absolute monarchy reared on the spoliation of the Church, the annexation of ecclesiastical jurisdiction, and the policy of blood and terror which compelled obedience. To him must be attributed as well some of the credit that rightly belongs to the statecraft of those years in another matter. Not content with building up the new monarchy in England, Cromwell had wider plans. Supremacy in England was not enough. The whole island must, if possible, be reduced to obedience. As early as 1533—and then, indeed, not before it was time—Cromwell was contemplating the discipline of Wales. The appearance in 1534 of Roland Lee as president of the council of the marches initiated something like a reign of terror in the country, and his reports to Cromwell resulted, in 1534, in legislation for tightening up the administrative control of the country with a view to decreasing the prevalent lawlessness. In 1536 an act incorporating Wales and England took up work which had been begun as early as Edward I. English legal procedure, laws and customs, were introduced, representa-

tion in the English parliament was granted, and
a thorough reorganization of the administrative
machinery was taken in hand. The work was
completed by another act of 1543, and one of the
first extensions of English sovereignty had been
achieved.

Ireland presented a worse problem, but here,
too, the principle of the consolidation of the royal
power was sought. The condition of Ireland
under Henry VII. will best be visualized by re-
calling the fact that most of the rebellions of that
reign could reckon on assistance from that country,
and despite the Poynings' administration, Ireland
remained a difficult problem for Tudor statesmen.
In 1528 the land was a field for Spanish intrigue,
and by 1534 it was in a state of wild rebellion.
In 1537 a commission was sent to deal with the
lawlessness. By 1541 some approach to better
government had been made, and by 1542 the
king's supremacy had been enforced, the English
judicial system had been planted in the country,
and there was some hope of a transitory peace.

Thus in all ways the career of Thomas Cromwell
suggests the main features of the policy of the later
years of the reign of Henry VIII. By his loyal
service, his ruthless execution of schemes Machiavellian in their subtlety, and his concentration upon
the assertion of royal supremacy, Cromwell made
Henry master in England. But he paid the penalty
of success. His policy was unpopular, and if
monarchy was to be saved, a scapegoat had to be
forthcoming. Cromwell, like Wolsey, had to play
the rôle of the sacrificed minister. The view that

would depict him as the victim of a blunder over the Cleves marriage is only half true. Henry undoubtedly turned against him for this marriage policy, which placed the king in the ridiculous situation of an unwilling bridegroom ; but there was more in Cromwell's ruin than this explanation suggests. Cromwell fell because he had contributed all he could towards Henry's greatness. To keep him in office after that was dangerous for the kingship. Thomas Cromwell, Earl of Essex, was executed on July 28, 1540, in order that Henry's popularity might be saved. It is hard to sympathize with him. None could possibly have known better than Cromwell the dangers of the game he played, and the cruel realism of even the best of his work makes it easier to sympathize with the victims of the terror than with the man who was primarily responsible for it.

One thing should be said in conclusion. Cromwell was the last of the great ministers of the reign. From his death until the death of Henry himself in 1547 there was little more great work to be done. Royal supremacy had been achieved. All that was now necessary was to work it in the interests of the monarch who was the head in State and Church.

CHAPTER VIII

THE DESPOTISM IN ACTION

WHEN the second Tudor monarch died in
1547, the framework of English governmental institutions had been erected. The influence of the changes which had been made
would remain in English history for centuries
after the dynasty that made them had passed
away. The greatness of those achievements is not
to be appreciated by a hasty glance ; much of the
comment often made upon them is confined to a
mere narrative of a series of royal activities ; the
full meaning of what was going on is often hidden
behind lists of statutes and tables of dates. Yet,
behind these minutiæ lies an important truth. A
form of government was being evolved whose
influence upon the lives of individuals was a
reality it is hardly possible to exaggerate, and if a
true picture of the conditions under which men
were living is to be obtained, it can only be by a
recognition of the intimate connection between the
individual and the machinery of government that
had come into existence.

The task is so difficult that it has been necessary
to coin a special phrase to describe the policy of the
dynasty with which we are dealing. The rule of

members of that dynasty was so personal, so intimately bound up with popular sympathy, that it stands out as a thing unique in English history. It was a form of government so peculiar that no one political term would fit it without some qualification. It was not a despotism in the full sense that word usually implies, for it had too many of the forms, at any rate, of constitutional monarchy. But there is something to be said for a description of it as a qualified absolutism, and the phrase Tudor despotism will, indeed, suggest its characteristics better than any other phrase.

That it was government with the essentials of despotism is best realized by a glance at the position of the king. Henry VII. had succeeded in establishing his position : Henry VIII. was busied with the task of decking it out with all the trappings of majesty. He was King and Pope : supreme in Church and State. His parliaments spoke of the King's Majesty in terms of lowliest deference. They petitioned their Most Rightful and Dreadful Sovereign Lord, and spoke mystically of " the royal estate of his imperial crown and dignity of Supreme Head of the Church of England." Nor were such expressions mere empty phrases. Parliament as the representative of the nation showed its feelings not merely by assisting and acquiescing in the fundamental changes in Church and State which have occupied so considerable a part of this narrative. In addition, it added very considerably to the powers of the monarch. Legislation on treason increased the number of the offences coming under that head. The supremacy of the

State over the Church was specially recognized in a Treason Act of 1536 and another of 1543, which made it a treasonable offence to deprive the king and other members of the royal family of the accumulation of titles and degrees collected around the throne during the course of the changes. Parliament was equally generous on the question lying so near the root of all Tudor troubles. It helped Henry to determine the succession by allowing him to work out his own desires. By the first Succession Act of 1534 it confirmed the marriage of Anne Boleyn, and gave the crown to her issue. In 1536 parliament annulled this arrangement in favour of the Seymour marriage, and failing the entail there arranged, Henry was empowered to devise the crown by will or letters patent. In 1543, when the problem was still unsolved, parliament passed another Succession Act dealing with the claims of Edward, Mary, and Elizabeth ; but if the arrangements then made failed, Henry was to continue to have the right of devising the crown by will.

Nor does this list exhaust the new powers granted to the king. By the Statute of Proclamations (1539), it was declared that proclamations issued by the king and council should have the force of law. The significance of this measure has often been exaggerated ; but in the reaction from such an extreme its importance can easily be lost. It is true that the issue of royal proclamations was not a novelty, and that the field specially covered by this act concerned heresy. Nevertheless, the importance of the statute lies in the parliamentary authority it gave for a practice which was not new, and it is another illustration of the powers definitely entrusted to the Tudor dynasty by parliament.

The new powers of the crown were exercised through the extremely efficient system of government that was at last beginning to work. In the reformed council which Henry VII. had done so much to strengthen, Henry VIII. found an agent that was rapidly developed to serve his purposes. His work was to systematize the plans of his father, to increase the proportion of men of lowly origin and official position within it, and to add to the duties ascribed to it in the reign of Henry VII. Under the second Tudor the council became firmly established as the nucleus of the central government, and it began to exercise functions that tended to increase with the passing of the years, until the Tudor council stands out as the supreme feature of the form of government peculiar to that dynasty. It is difficult to describe those functions in a way at once accurate and brief. For the essence of conciliar activity lay in its ubiquity. No matter likely to be of importance in the state can be said to have been outside the sphere of its interference. The Tudor council was the body which gave the king the means for supervising and controlling all that was done in the country. Such functions suggest to the modern mind a body something in the nature of the cabinet ; but this would hardly be an accurate description of the Tudor institution. The advisory functions of the council were not its most important feature, for the

Tudors kept the control of important policy in their own hands. It was rather in its capacity as a body supervising the agents of the executive that the council really did its greatest work, and in it there remained judicial power which increased its prestige and its utility.

Closely connected with the council under Henry VII. had been the courts of star chamber and of requests. These bodies, developed by Wolsey, had proved invaluable, and they were further strengthened to carry out their work in the later years of the reign. More than this, the success of their exercise of a judicial power had been so beneficial for the maintenance of law and order that the principle on which they were based was used for extensions. Conciliar judicial administration was applied to purposes that might almost be summed up as local government. The work of the council was decentralized. Thus a council for the north—of which there are traces before Henry VIII.'s time—was definitely at work under a president in 1530, and became a permanent body in 1537. It was established to deal with the lawlessness of the Border country, and its function was to apply a kind of star chamber government in those parts of the country not easily accessible to the officials of the court at Westminster. In the same way, and in order to deal with similar problems, a council of Wales—growing out of the council of the Prince of Wales—was given statutory powers in 1531, and became a jurisdictional body in 1543. The disorder in the western counties, which came to a head in the insurrection of 1537, led to a similar organization —the council of the west. It was modelled on the other conciliar courts, but its history is obscure, and its main interest comes from the conviction with which contemporaries held that such an administrative form had justified its existence by the work done in other parts of the country.

The importance and utility of this conciliar method of government is further revealed by the ease with which it was applied in order to work out some of the changes which followed as a result of the Reformation. Thus, for instance, the financial administration made inevitable by ecclesiastical changes was dealt with by conciliar courts. In 1536 a court of augmentations was set up to deal with the problems arising from the sequestration of ecclesiastical lands, and to handle the revenue accruing from them. A similar court was established in 1540 to account for the first-fruits and tenths falling to the king, while the court of wards and liveries, established in 1540, was intended to administer the property of the king's wards. In 1542 a court of surveyors was given the task of looking after royal property. Such exploitation of the idea of conciliar courts points to the success of the new agent of government, and that success, in turn, helps to explain why the Tudors were popular rulers.

A central organization of this nature kept the government in touch with the political problems arising in all parts of the country. The system was further strengthened by what was to become a distinctive feature of Tudor organization. The efficiency of government rests ultimately on the realization of a full control over local government, and it was the peculiar success of the Tudor despotism in achieving that control which gives the period a special claim to attention. To have solved that momentous problem is itself adequate justification for the existence of the despotism. The means whereby contact between the central government and local government was achieved is in itself a subject for a lengthy work, and it must be sufficient if we simply indicate the clue to the answer. In their search for an efficient liaison officer, the Tudors alighted on the justice of the peace, and in the hands of Henry VIII. and his successors that officer became an indispensable part of the machinery of government. The justice of the peace was the office boy of the Tudor monarchy, and his duties can only be satisfactorily summed up—as one historian has aptly said—by putting them under all the letters of the alphabet. Here it will be enough to say that to him fell the task of putting into operation most of the statutes and proclamations flowing in a steady stream throughout the period from the central government. Without the justice of the peace local administration would have come to a standstill, and the efficiency of the Tudor despotism depended more on the local patriotism of the justices than on any other single factor. To their activity English history owed a debt only a historian of the Stuart period can rightly appreciate. For it was in the ever-increasing work of the sessions, and in the manifold variety of administrative duties attendant upon the office, that the country gentlemen of Tudor England learned the art of government. When the time came they showed that they knew how to put that knowledge to the best of uses.

Thus was carried to its logical conclusion that policy of consolidation upon which Henry VII. had lavished so much care. By means of it there was set up an administration which may rightly be pointed out as the unique achievement of government in Europe in the sixteenth century, and that result goes far to explain the success of Henry VII. and his successors. That does not, however, explain everything. Machinery such as this would be sufficient to explain the establishment of a despotism. It is not enough to explain the Tudor despotism, for it fails to take into account the Tudors. Whatever estimate may be made of the characters of Henry VII. and Henry VIII., there can be no gainsaying that they both possessed qualities which made them peculiarly fitted to govern England at a crucial period in its history. They restored to the kingship that which had been lacking for a long period, for they were efficient monarchs who knew their duties, and gave the impression that they were competent to govern the country. They inspired confidence, and they came as saviours of society after the chaos created by a series of rulers who had failed to become masters of the state. Something more than mere efficiency gave them their ascendancy. They embodied national aspirations, and seemed instinctively able to understand the people over whom they had been called to rule. Thus they were able to cast their plans into forms acceptable to the people, and by skilful management they succeeded in winning and keeping the support of their subjects even when their schemes involved dangers not lightly to be undertaken by any nation. It is this harmony between king and subjects that is the true explanation of the Tudor despotism. For the system of government thus established was unique, not because it was an absolute rule exercised by one man over cowed and terrorized subjects, but because it was a government in which the ruler was the representative of national ideas and hopes. There were moments, indeed, when terrorism is almost the right word to apply to the government of the country, but those moments were not typical. On the whole, it is just to say that the English people were behind most of the changes taking place, and the success of Henry VIII.'s policy can never be explained on the assumption that he drove obstinately towards his goal without the sympathy and the support of his subjects. He could never have achieved what he did without support. Hence the truth that, as a matter of strict fact, no despotism in the literal sense of that word was established. Tudor despotism is yet another example of the spirit of compromise in which the English people have always delighted to approach their problems. Just as the ultimate solution of monarchy was to be found in England in a form of limited kingship, so despotism, when established, had to take the shape of a limited (or Tudor) despotism.

The factor which explains the limitation of

despotism was, of course, parliament, and no true estimate of the system of government established in sixteenth-century England would be accurate without a realization of the place occupied by that institution in the political life of the time. To those who are accustomed to think of parliament as the central feature of the constitution, it will probably seem strange that so much should have been said about the agents of government in Tudor England before dealing with what they must regard as the prime agent, and in their scale of values a description of parliament ought to have come first. To take back such a scale of values into Tudor England is to make an explanation of Tudor despotism impossible. Parliament came to be a necessary part of the constitutional machinery of this country, but its growth was slow, and it is because of the deftness of their touch in dealing with this institution that the Tudors deserve their greatest credit as administrators. For the theme of parliamentary history during this period was as simple as it was important. The period began with parliament occupying an insignificant place in the organization of government. It was at first a body rarely called, and often not consulted on many of the really important matters of policy. The work of Henry VIII. was to give it greater prestige, more freedom to speak its own mind, a greater share in the shaping of policy and the work of government. The change was deliberate. Henry realized the weakness of Wolsey's autocratic attitude towards parliament, and his own great love of legalism made him aware of the advantages to be gained from the demonstration of national support that would be revealed if his policy were expressed in acts of parliament. Thus he went carefully to work to obtain parliamentary sanction for the changes he introduced in Church and State. Cromwell proved an able assistant in such work. The dangers attendant upon sharing his policy with the commons were not as real as they appear to be on the surface. For in the last resort the influence of the crown over the representatives of the country was at all times considerable. The legislation submitted to the House was drafted by royal servants, so that the crown could control it. The speaker was a royal official, whose salary was paid by the king. Many, if not all, of the councillors were also members of parliament, so that they were able to supervise royal interests, and could influence the course of action in parliament. Even in the composition of the House there were some traces of influence exercised on behalf of the Crown, but such influence must not be exaggerated. There were some instances of interference in elections—Cromwell was an offender—and by means of royal letters a constituency could occasionally be influenced in the cause of the king. And yet when all is said, it seems fair to conclude that the early Tudors did little to pack parliament. They could be sure of support for most of the policy they wished to work out, and the opposition of parliament was not so vital as to need elaborate methods for overcoming it.

It would be wrong, then, to treat of the Tudor

parliament as an institution corresponding to a modern assembly. It sat on rare occasions, and members were only too anxious to get their work done quickly in order to return to their homes. So much was this the case that in 1515 Henry VIII. found it necessary to pass an act enforcing attendance upon members by preventing them from absenting themselves before the end of the parliament unless they had special permission from the speaker and the Commons. The penalty for unlicensed departure was to be the forfeiture of the wages due to the member. The Tudors did not call parliaments more often than they could help. In his reign of twenty-four years Henry VII. only called seven parliaments ; and in thirty-eight years Henry VIII. only held nine. Between 1515 and 1523 no parliament was called, and even the important Reformation Parliament sat in short sessions and at irregular intervals. The parliaments of Edward VI. and Mary were governed by these traditions.

This infrequency of parliamentary sessions was important. It meant that the government of the country did not come under the control of parliament to anything like the extent familiar to those accustomed to think of a legislative assembly meeting regularly and for long sessions. During the periods when parliament did not meet, the government of the country was in the hands of the council. It was the executive that was the really important agent of government. Even when parliament was sitting it was not able to make its power fully felt. For the long intervals that elapsed between sessions meant that members had little chance of forming an organized opposition. They did not get to know each other sufficiently well to work together. Naturally, under such conditions, the crown had all advantages on its side. The Tudors could afford to give parliament considerable freedom of action, for they retained in their own hands sufficient powers to enable them to check any signs of the growth of too independent an attitude.

These considerations must not, however, be used to form too clear-cut a picture of Tudor parliaments as completely subservient to the crown. Despite all the influences making for royal control, parliament still enjoyed considerable freedom, and the view that the revolutionary changes of the period were forced upon an unwilling but subservient institution which had been terrorized into submission is false. If Henry is condemned for the changes of his reign, the indictment must be drawn against the parliament as well as against the king, since the changes introduced were supported by members. Had this not been the case there might have been different results. There were occasions when the parliament could undoubtedly have gone further than it did in opposition, were it not perfectly clear that it supported the royal policy. On occasions parliament could be self-willed. The measure which is usually—though not justly—regarded as the high-water mark of parliamentary subservience, the Statute of Proclamations, is an interesting case in point. The first draft of that act went through three readings in the House of Lords. It was then considerably " reformed," and sent to the Commons. They threw out the Bill, and passed a new one to take its place. This, after amendment by the Lords, was passed. Something more than the royal will was being expressed in the Statute of Proclamations, and the act is a better test of the country's confidence in the Tudor dynasty than it is of royal autocracy in dealings with parliaments. Other instances might be given to prove that parliament rejected measures with which it did not agree, and if the legislation of this period is to be understood, it must be recognized that the legislature was prepared to support Henry in most of the things he did.

There is no difficulty in understanding the relations between the Tudors and their parliaments provided sufficient emphasis is placed upon the Tudors themselves. In the qualities common to all of them lies much of the explanation of their success. They were new monarchs of a singular type. They were popular, and they had a political gift of the utmost importance. They were able to keep their fingers on the national pulse, and they were clever enough to moderate their policy to accord with the fluctuations of the national will. Thus they gained and kept the support of their subjects. The secret of the new despotism lay there. By means of that support Henry VIII. was able to work his will on State and Church, and the work he did supplied problems that were to remain for future generations to solve. When the full meaning of Henry's policy has been grasped, it will be seen that the remainder of the Tudor period—and not a little of the Stuart period as well—was spent in working out the implications of his work.

In the sphere of politics Henry's main contribution had been the new conception of monarchy. The king stood high above his subjects in a way true of no previous period in English history. He maintained his position by a combination never previously possible. The new middle class, emerging out of the wreckage of feudalism, was the hope of the future, and in allying with this class rather than with an effete aristocracy, Henry was responsible for a new orientation in politics. The significance of this alliance was to be the key to later history. The king, who did most for the building up of his own absolutism, supplied also the limitations to that power. When the time came, that middle class, which owed so much to the results of his work, proved strong enough to check the further growth of the power of the crown. It was able to do so because, under the Tudors, it was given wealth and political training. The dissolution of the monasteries and the transference of land consequent upon it provided much of the former, the growth of parliament and the training of the justices of the peace provided the latter. But under the Tudors that day had not yet arrived. The great contribution of the new monarchy to the theory and practice of politics was the new concept of the kingship, and the fresh ideas of the nature of the State which it developed.

It is in this period that the idea of the supremacy of the State became a governing motive of politics. The interests of that institution became the end of all government, its welfare transcended in importance the welfare of individuals, its actions were unquestionable, its powers unchallengeable. For it men lived. For it they were prepared to die. In a word, the Leviathan of Hobbes was being fashioned. That philosopher wrote his treatise on government in Stuart times, but it was the Tudor State he was describing, and the words which he used were those a Tudor politician might have penned. The Tudor State was indeed " that great ' leviathan,' or rather, to speak more reverently . . . that ' mortal god ' to which we owe, under the ' immortal God,' our peace and defence."

These new ideas had been planted. For good and evil they were to come to harvest in the future, and the immediate sequel to Henry's reign is of interest because it was the period when it became clear that the new plants had struck root. Henry's State, Henry's King—these were strange creations, and they would have to stand the test of time. The reigns of Edward VI. and Mary put them to a test more serious than their most cunning enemy could have invented for them. For the Tudor despotism had to show its strength under the least promising of conditions. It had to face, in the first place, the rule of a child, and then it had to be given over into the hands of a woman who was a fanatic. In the Middle Ages such tests were almost inevitably fatal to all hope of good government. The final justification of the despotism of the early Tudors is that that organization proved strong enough to stand the strain each of these casualties put upon it. Not only so. When both emergencies had been met, it still remained so strong that when another woman ascended the throne it turned her into a king.

Henry's reign opened up problems along another line, for the English Reformation in his reign had not by any means solved a religious question common to all Europe. Indeed, what had been done so far simply proved the existence of difficulties that would some day have to be faced. Henry's work had delivered a shattering blow to many traditional ideas. The theory of a universal Church had become an impossible ideal for England, and the sovereignty of the Pope in this country had been trampled into the dust. But these changes, as we have seen, had not been accompanied by any important innovations in doctrine. There existed, as a consequence of this deficiency, a number of anomalies which sooner or later would have to be corrected, and the problems of the future lay along the line of doctrinal change. They were problems that would not allow of any simple solution. For, in the first place, the Church of Rome was still powerful. It had not by any means abandoned hope of winning back the English people to itself. And, in the second place, the revolutionary party within the country, stimulated by the policy of Henry VIII. and by active contact with continental Protestantism, was growing daily in numbers and enthusiasm. The new doctrinal settlement would have to be hammered out on the anvil of compromise, so as to defeat the disintegrating influences of both these extreme parties. It was work not likely to be accomplished in a day, nor could it have been successfully undertaken had there not been a strong government in command of England. That necessity the Tudor despotism was able to supply.

The reader who has begun to peer into the future, across the grave of Henry VIII., should be recognizing some of these as the problems of vital significance in the political and religious life of England. In what spirit they were met, and how they were solved, it must be the work of succeeding chapters to indicate.

CHAPTER IX

THE RETURN OF FACTION

IT will be appreciated from what has been already said that mere length of time is a poor standard wherewith to measure Tudor history, but the warning is one that will bear repetition as a prelude to the study of Edwardian history. By such a test the reign of Edward VI. will hardly appear important, while that of his successor, Mary, is of slightly shorter length, since Edward only reigned from 1547 to 1553, and Mary's tragedy was done by 1558. Ten years of Tudor history, however, could work enormous change. Speaking without too strict an interpretation of accuracy, it may be said that ten years saw the vital changes of the Reformation an accomplished fact, and that another ten sufficed to place the despotism on a firm foundation. What might not the decade after Henry's death bring forth? The answer should be pondered, for in it lies the summing up of Henry's work.

What was passing through the minds of the statesmen in charge of affairs is clearly mirrored in their actions after the death of Henry. He died on January 28, 1547. For three days those who knew were afraid to tell the nation. They saw quite plainly the difficulties that must instantly arise. Indeed, Henry himself had spared some attention to the problem, and had even fancied he knew the way to solve it. For it seemed to one who was, to all intents and purposes, the State in England, and who had been strong enough to trample papal claims into the dust, that yet another proof of sovereign power might be shown the world before he had to leave his throne. Henry believed he could cheat death of its victory. So he settled the succession, carefully arranged the personnel and the form the government should take after his death, and then departed, thinking he could still rule England from the tomb. It was not to be. The theme of Edward's reign was to be the shaking free of England from the grip of the dead hand.

The feature of paramount interest in the new reign was that the new monarch was a little child. From that followed everything else. The royal minority meant that there was no strong king to take up the responsibilities imposed upon the kingship by the new despotism, and as a result England was back again in the position where she had stood when Henry VII. rescued her from the chaos of the fifteenth century. The stage was set for the old drama. True, indeed, enormous changes had taken place since 1485, but the question still wanting an answer was whether they were sufficient to make the old drama impossible. The crucial point was that the Tudor despotism had its *raison d'être* in a reality no longer in existence. It depended entirely on the strong

king. Could the system work without its natural
head ? The outlook was not promising. The
minor king had no will of his own. It was impossible to guess whether the world in general
would accept the things that would have to be
done by others in his name. It was not even
certain whether such assent would be forthcoming
in England.

Almost as important was the fact that the royal
helplessness implied a need for some form of
guidance, but the problem to settle was what form
such guidance was to take. The answer was uncertain. Henry VIII.'s solution was the obvious
one of a council of regency ; but the question
Henry never settled was whether such a council
could possibly work. Much has already been
said about the Tudor council, and Henry's choice
of this method of government is an indirect com-
pliment to the efficiency of that body during his
lifetime. It should, however, be noticed that
every argument in praise of Henry's council is
really an additional argument against its utility
in the conditions of the new reign. Henry's
council, as we have seen, was to a great extent
successful because it had no will of its own, and
even if it had shown signs of possessing one, it
would never have been allowed, much less have
been called upon, to use it. Its function was to
carry out Henry's policy. Now a council responsible for thinking out a policy, as well as for
administering it, was a body very different from
the council Henry knew. The question was
whether the men named for Edward's council

could rise to such demands. Henry seemed to think so, though he was clever enough to see the dangers ahead and to take steps against them. He tried to make the new body one which would carry out a policy such as he would himself have developed, and for this purpose he arranged for a council the majority of whose members were on the side of reform. It was probably a wiser policy than one of compromise would have been, for a division of practically equal parties within the council would not have been practicable. Perfect balance could not be attained, and it is very much open to question whether it would have been desirable even if it could have been attained. For its sole result must inevitably have been sterility. Once the likelihood of supremacy by one or other party is admitted, the way in which further difficulties would arise must be clear. There was no constitutional arrangement for a government opposition within the council, so the only move open to the beaten party would be to become a faction. It followed, therefore, that the centre of interest within the council was bound to be the person chosen to act as regent.

Much might be written on the need for, and advantages of, the office of regent, but it is more important to notice that the office has nearly always had two serious disadvantages. They completely outweigh all to be said in its favour. The first of them is that no regent has ever convinced all of his contemporaries that he is the ideal man for the office, and that leads to competition for the position. The second is that the regent is faced by such great temptations to make himself king that few men have ever been able to withstand them, and that leads to usurpation, sometimes to civil war, and in some circumstances to the establishment of a new dynasty.

At the accession of Edward VI., then, England was faced with all the possibilities similar conditions had produced in the later Middle Ages. And all those possibilities were destined to become realities. In Protector Somerset there was a regent unable to get a firm grip on the tasks of government, and consequently unable to win unanimous sympathy in the country. In Northumberland there was the unscrupulous rival scheming for greater power, who would end by becoming a king-maker. In Lady Jane Grey there was the puppet who was to be the means for achieving Northumberland's aims and establishing a new dynasty on the throne. In Edward VI. there was the helpless victim of advisers who brought into English politics the family feuds of the wars of the roses. In a word, the reign of Edward VI. is thick with the atmosphere of the fifteenth century. And yet, history was not about to repeat itself. The chaotic conditions of the fifteenth century did not entirely return. If we seek the reason we shall learn more about the success of Henry VIII.'s work than we can hope to discover if we make a study which ends with his death.

In Somerset the least unattractive personality of the conflict is to be seen. High in Henry VIII.'s favour, brother of Jane Seymour, and therefore uncle to her son Edward, he was the obvious candidate for the office of regent. In January 1547 he became protector and governor of the young king. From 1547–49 he retained control, but in that short period his policy evoked such criticism that he could not stand against the plots of Northumberland. After that, until his death, the rivalry of these two men shaped the politics of England. Somerset, during his period of office, failed because in part he could not, and in part he would not, wield the powers of a Henry VIII. He believed that more was to be gained by leniency than by terror, and he sought to relieve the stringency of Henry's rule by a more liberal policy. Thus a less severe attitude towards extreme reform prevailed, and Henry's vigorous control of heresy and treason was allowed to lapse. It was a fatal mistake. It gave an opportunity to the disorderly elements within the state that were ready to turn liberty into licence. Thus leniency was thought to be weakness, and the leaders of revolution—and reaction—within State and Church fought to make good their plans.

Somerset possessed many of the qualities of the true idealist. He was sympathetic to the difficulties caused by the agrarian and social questions, whose importance during this period will call for attention at another place, but his philanthropic schemes only served to arouse against him the prosperous middle class, which had nothing to gain and much to lose by the encouragement of schemes such as these. Against their opposition he failed to make good. He was a man of wide

views, but the difficulties against which he laboured
were too great for him. If he could have had his
way the imperial policy of Henry VIII. and
Cromwell would have been worked out to the full
by the incorporation of Scotland. Unfortunately
he had no practical policy. Circumstances forced
him to war, but the battle of Pinkie (1547) was
a wasteful tragedy. A battle could not solve the
Scottish problem, and Somerset could not see his
way clearly enough to embark upon a consistent
policy calculated to lead to practical results.
Scotland, worked upon by France, remained a
problem which was to go unsolved until the end
of the Tudor period. Somerset's religious ideals
were not popular, and the movements towards
reform which marked his protectorate only led to
increased opposition to his rule. As a statesman
he was not without ideals, but he lacked practical
aims, and there were in him defects of character
which lost him many friends. With all his faults,
however, he was infinitely to be preferred to most
of his contemporaries, and he is supremely
attractive when compared with the rival at whose
hands he was to suffer death.

In John Dudley, Earl of Warwick and later
Duke of Northumberland, Protector Somerset
had a rival who was the incarnation of the self-
seeking of his age. Son of that Dudley notorious
under Henry VII., he was the second generation
of the new type produced by Henry VII.'s statesmanship. He brought into the politics of the reign
all the vices of the new generation and many of
those of the fifteenth century as well. After the

fall of Somerset in October 1549, he rose to power.
At first he appeared simply as a member of the
council, but he was aiming at greater influence.
His plans represent an ever-increasing audacity.
In February 1550 Somerset was released from the
Tower, and once at large he was an object of
suspicion to Northumberland, who feared that
intrigue would give his rival a party strong enough
to thwart his own plans. The aim of Northumberland was to get rid of Somerset. This was
achieved by packing the council, and by hindering
any summons of parliament, since that body might
quite probably support Somerset. By December
1551 Northumberland's plots for the downfall
of his rival were successful. An alleged conspiracy against Northumberland and the king was
concocted as a charge against him. The trial
was managed, and in January 1552 Somerset was
executed. After that event the schemes of Northumberland can be seen in full light. He tried to
hide his unpopularity by a return to the policy of
terror, and under the cloak of religion he sought
his own ends. It looked as though he was likely
to succeed, and the period of his power was one
in which the comparative tolerance of Somerset's
policy was lost. The ruthlessness of Northumberland's schemes was dangerous, and he was
forced to safeguard himself by winning the
support of the king. By 1550 he was doing
what he could to gain an ascendancy over the
young Edward. In August he tried to dispense
with the phrase " by advice of the council " in
documents signed by the king, and in August 1551

there came the suggestion that Edward, then
thirteen years of age, should sit in the council.
The young king's journal proves that he had
ability—and the unlovely qualities of the dynasty
of which he was a member—so that the scheme
was less ridiculous than might appear at first sight.
Unfortunately for Northumberland he was faced
by a rival more deadly than Somerset. Disease
had Edward in its grip, and the end could not be
long delayed. It needed little prescience to see
that Edward's grave would hold the ruins of
Northumberland's plans. That was the motive
for Northumberland's gamble on higher stakes.
If control could not be retained through Edward,
then he must control Edward's successor. He
set up as a king-maker. The plan he had in mind
made it essential that his king should be a queen,
for he thought he could best assure his future
by means of a marriage alliance in his own house.
He married Guilford Dudley, his fourth son, to
Lady Jane Grey, daughter of Frances, Duchess
of Suffolk, and granddaughter of Mary, the wife
of Charles Brandon, Duke of Suffolk. Jane
was therefore the granddaughter of the sister of
Henry VIII., and Northumberland's scheme was
to get the throne for her. He prepared to play
on Edward's undoubted Protestant sympathies.
The young king was persuaded to arrange the
succession in favour of the party of reform.
After Edward's death the plot was carried out,
and on July 10, 1553, Lady Jane was proclaimed
queen. It was a desperate experiment, doomed
to failure. After all, the Tudor despotism was

not to be thrown away in exchange for the anarchy of the wars of the roses. Northumberland, deserted by his own party, was ultimately forced to proclaim Mary Tudor as queen, on July 20, 1553. He did not escape the consequences of his acts. On August 22, 1553, he went the way Somerset had gone. Even at the scaffold this desperate gambler could not resist a throw with death. He staked everything upon a recantation. It was an action pleasing to the government, but it did not bring him the pardon he had hoped. Its sole result was to convince his contemporaries that his policy had been as insincere as it had been selfish. To the lengthy indictment against him one last charge must be added. His unscrupulous plots had not even the merit of giving England a strong government. He was a failure.

If, on the one hand, the reign of Edward is of interest as a proof that the Tudor despotism could survive conditions which had broken dynasties in the fifteenth century, it was, on the other hand, a melancholy reminder of the price England was paying for the new order. It was during this reign that there began to be felt the full effects of economic movements whose existence during the early years of the Tudor period has been so far completely ignored. The only justification for such an omission is that it was in the reign of Edward VI. that the full impact of the movement was felt, and thus a favourable opportunity is provided for studying the ultimate effect of changes whose influence had been accumulating throughout the reigns of his predecessors.

It has become the fashion in modern histories to belittle the effects of the economic disorganization of England in the sixteenth century. As in the case of most reactions from accepted views, however, it is possible to go too far in the opposite direction. Little will be gained by trying to blot out of English history the fact that the new England, rising out of the old in the early years of the sixteenth century, was the victim of serious attacks of growing pains. For the answer to any denial of the gravity of the changes is to be found in some data not easily disproved. The period under review saw a number of serious risings of the population, and these must be largely attributed to the discontent consequent on social and economic change. Further, contemporary writers were eloquent in the criticisms they levelled against the new order, and most of them agree in deploring the changes they saw going on around them as they wrote. All this suggests that those competent to express their ideas on paper during this period were impressed by the disturbances with which they were familiar. Lastly, the legislation of the period shows a number of acts intended to deal specifically with some of these economic difficulties. This is a sufficient indication that the problem was serious enough to warrant the intervention of the government. Now, it is true that these rebellions were not entirely due to economic movements. Other factors, especially dissatisfaction with the religious innovations, also had their place in bringing about the prevailing unrest. It is not, however, unfair to state that the economic factor played the greater part in bringing the troubles to a head. In the same way, the pamphlet literature of the period can be ascribed to violent partisanship on the part of extremists. There is much truth in such a statement, but there is not enough to explain it wholly away. Some reality lay behind the accounts of the distress which these writers alleged was the result of the economic disturbances of the time. They were, in part at any rate, the expression of definite impressions familiar to readers of their works, and if we accept the moderating tendencies of some modern research we must take care that generalizations are not made too sweeping. Real grievances, serious economic disturbances, were behind the expressions of discontent to be found without much search in the literature of the reigns of Henry VIII. and Edward VI.

What was happening was that the mediæval structure of economic life was slowly subsiding before men's eyes. The subsidence was gradual. It did not affect all parts of the country to an equal extent, nor was its full meaning realized by all the men of the time. Changes were nevertheless taking place, and in the face of such changes it would have been little consolation for the sufferers to be told that they formed only a small proportion of the population, and that economic disturbance was not adversely affecting all members of the community. The tragedy of the situation was that it was the very poor who suffered most acutely, and while—from one standpoint—we may look out across an England of prosperity and progress, another viewpoint will reveal dark patches on the landscape. The rich were growing richer, the poor were becoming poorer. The pressure of economic forces was driving the less fortunate members of society deeper and deeper below the subsistence line. No picture of Tudor England would approximate to the truth were these shadows not shown, and what follows is an attempt to sketch in the merest outline some of the factors making for misery and discontent in an England where the strong hand of the Tudor despotism was producing so many beneficial results.

The Black Death (1348–49) had hastened a dissolution of mediæval society, but the ultimate results of the disintegration that had begun before that event were not to be fully appreciated until Tudor times. Shortage of labour, and the resultant economic disturbances which such shortage inevitably produced, had set in motion an agricultural revolution which lightened the burdens of the labouring class, and, by freeing lands from feudal ties, increased the number of yeomen. The growth of the woollen industry brought wealth to the merchant class, and that wealth produced capital for more expansion. The immediate result was an increased demand for raw material, and sheep-farming became a venture which ensured a solid return to the speculator. Such a development led to a rapid change in economic organization. The self-sufficing village community made contact with a larger world. A new orientation of economic and commercial interests was established.

The reorganization of the Tudor period hastened the crisis by supplying new factors influencing this general movement. The decline of the feudal aristocracy and the war upon maintenance and livery meant the dispersal of retainers and the family servants of the great houses. Thomas More in his *Utopia* had been quick to see what this meant. As he says, many of these men were soldiers, untrained in the arts of peace, and when they found it difficult to get employment—as they usually did—they were quickly transformed into the lawless vagrants who were a nuisance to the peace-abiding citizen. While they were being forced into the ranks of an army of outcast poor, the work of the government was reacting to the benefit of other, more fortunate, members of society. Peace brought prosperity to the middle class, and gave them a higher standard of living, while security resulted in an increased population. The inevitable result was a rise in prices, and what was beneficial for the few became a source of greater distress for the many. The dissolution of the monasteries and the raid on gild funds, while not as grave a factor in the poverty problem as used to be supposed, had nevertheless serious results. The consequent redistribution of land quickened the spirit of commercialism, and encouraged the middleman speculating in the purchase and re-sale of leases at an exorbitant profit. The squandering of the wealth which should have remained in the hands of the crown left the government still searching for ways of increasing the revenue. A cruel expedient was found in the debasement of the coinage. Henry VIII. taught contemporaries this mean trick, and there were five successive tamperings with the currency between the years 1527 and 1551. The criminality of such a proceeding will not need any emphasis if it is remembered that any interference with the purity of the coinage is, by the very nature of things, a blow at the poorest of subjects. Little wonder that when an economist views the period, with his eyes more open to economic effects than to religious or constitutional developments, his judgment on the author of such a policy should be bitter. Thus, Thorold Rogers, on the strength of Henry VIII.'s currency policy, had no hesitation in denouncing that monarch as " the Vitellius and Nero of English history." It is so bitter a verdict that many will be tempted to dismiss it as an exaggeration worth little attention. The thoughtful reader will not allow its rich vituperation to go entirely waste. He will use it to modify the impression of a patriot king provided for him in Froude's *History*.

The key problem of the economic life of the times was the enclosure movement. For general purposes it is sufficient to remember that enclosure meant the fencing of land so as to vest it in an individual as absolute owner. By this means the land was set free from any rights—such as that of common—which hindered the full exploitation of the land for purposes of cultivation. To condemn the whole of that change, which was consolidating the holdings of mediæval agricultural economy, would be to misunderstand what was taking place. Much of the enclosure being made

201

was beneficial, for it improved husbandry and made possible new and improved methods of agriculture. But much that was done was done to promote sheep-farming. It involved consequences that were less praiseworthy. It often meant depopulation, and fed that spirit of self-seeking, fraught with appalling sufferings for the poor and the weak, which is the striking feature of the period. While it is true that the progress of the enclosure movement was nothing like as widespread as the lamentations of the pamphleteers suggest, it is also true that there was enough going on to promote hardship. Sir Thomas More's *Utopia* touched a raw spot in Tudor economic life when it attributed the evils of the period to the fact that " sheep were eating men." For the direct result of many of the enclosures was a displacement of population which resulted in unemployment and vagrancy. Early in the Tudor period the biggest social problem of the age—that of poverty—had become a menace to the community. Vagabonds and able-bodied beggars, unwilling to find work, kept company upon the roads of England with genuine victims of the prevailing unemployment, filled the towns, terrorized the peaceful dwellers in the country, and heaped up social difficulties that were not to be even partially solved until the Tudor period was drawing to its end. Despite the legislation of Henry VII., Wolsey, and Henry VIII., against enclosures, the movement went on, and by the end of the reign of Edward VI. discontent in the country was strong enough to find expression in a direct threat of rebellion. There had been earlier hints of what was likely to happen. In 1536 the Pilgrimage of Grace had shown what was to be expected when religious and economic grievances fused; but more dangerous outbursts were to come. In the reign of Edward VI. the pent-up discontent burst into a conflagration which called for all the energies of the government before it was extinguished.

Somerset made a brave stand. In 1548 he took the side of the poor by issuing a proclamation against enclosures, and by the appointment of a commission entrusted with the task of dealing with the agrarian problem. The gesture did not check the prevailing tendency towards open rebellion. In 1549 risings occurred in the West Country, spreading rapidly across towards Oxfordshire, Buckingham, Surrey, Sussex, and Kent. They were but the prelude to the more serious rising in Norfolk. There the rebels, under Robert Kett, a man not without lands and influence, definitely rose against the enclosures of common lands. They proceeded to break down the hedges, and making their headquarters at Mousehold Heath, near Norwich, began a campaign against neighbouring landowners. The movement was not entirely economic in character. None of these movements ever was. The innovations in the Church also had a share in the responsibility for what occurred. But a religio-political movement of this nature could not stop the prevailing tendencies in agrarian history. The rebellion was suppressed after heavy losses—3,500 of the rebels

are said to have been slain—the leaders were
hanged, and the discontented remnants found
themselves in no better plight than they had been
in before they took the remedy into their own
hands. Somerset's policy failed to arrest the
growing tide of discontent, and with his fall there
was introduced a policy of reaction. The parliament which met in November 1552 put into
operation a scheme which was not merely reac-
tionary, but was conceived in the bitterest spirit
of vindictiveness. Statutes enabled landlords to
enclose land when and however they liked, and
made it an offence to be visited with severe
penalties for their victims to offer any opposition.
Any meetings of the poor for the purposes of
reducing rents or prices were declared a felony.
It is not possible to blame parliament entirely for
these results. The drift towards enclosure was
wellnigh inevitable, for the force of the new economic movements could not be checked by legislation. But for the less fortunate members of
society to whom these changes were bound to
mean suffering, there was ample room for fierce
discontent. The prosperity that was undoubtedly
characteristic of the time, in which they quite as
undoubtedly had little share, gave them just title
to the grievances they ventilated.

The attempts made during this period to deal
with the grave social evils resulting from the
economic crisis through which England was passing are of deep interest. They reveal the government at work dealing with a problem assuming
serious proportions. It was not a new problem.

" The poor ye have always with you." But they were less passive at this period than they have been at some other times in our history, and the nature of their grievances was such as did not allow society completely to ignore their cries. Their existence was an undeniable fact confronting statesmen, and it was being borne in upon the minds of the best thinkers and politicians of the time that the problem of poverty was acquiring too serious a nature to be dealt with by the shiftless methods characteristic of earlier times. Slowly the State was being forced to accept some measure of responsibility for the ever-increasing class of destitute persons within its borders. The experiments that were made to deal with them may be likened to the gropings of a man in the dark. But the gropings were not made entirely in vain. In their stumblings statesmen happened upon some important truths. Slowly but surely they were being led towards a solution of the problem of poverty based on principles that were to govern English Poor Law administration for centuries. The first indications of the discovery of such principles provide an interesting line of study during the period with which this book is concerned.

The first legislation of the period dealing with poverty was the act of 1495. It did not go far. It sought to abolish poverty by calling the poor vagabonds, and by ordering their punishment and return to the districts whence they had come. Then, in 1531, the government took an important step in the direction of a more constructive policy. By an act of that year—the responsibility for administering it fell, of course, on the justice of the peace—an important principle was established. For this act drew a distinction between the different kinds of poor, dividing them into vagabonds and impotent poor, into work-shy and physically unfit. For the vagabonds the remedy suggested was punishment ; but it was beginning to be realized that those destitute through no fault of their own ought to be relieved. They were therefore permitted to beg, though only under certain restrictions. The distinction thus made was maintained in the act of 1536. Here, again, vagabonds and sturdy beggars were to be punished and forced to work. In dealing with the impotent poor, however, another idea was developed. An attempt was made to fix responsibility for the care of such unfortunates upon the parishes. Arrangements were made for the collection of voluntary alms to be used in the relief of this class.

The growth of the problem of poverty under Edward VI. resulted in further legislation, in which there was little sentimentality displayed. By an act of 1547 the punishment of vagabonds was made more severe. On conviction they were to be branded on the breast, and in hopeless cases they might be reduced to slavery for a period of two years. Repeated escapes were to end in death for felony. More enlightened was the treatment of the impotent poor. The scheme suggested in the act of 1536 was followed by an arrangement that in every parish collections should be taken on Sundays for the benefit of the destitute, and sermons should be preached calling upon those more plentifully provided with this world's goods to provide alms for their poorer neighbours. The last effort to be recorded here was the act of 1552. This had no new remedy for the problem of vagabondage, but it systematized the arrangements made for the other class of poor. Two collectors of alms were to be appointed yearly in every town and parish. They were to keep a register in which they were to enter the names of all who would promise contributions, while they were also to keep a list of the deserving poor. Each week they were to make grants of relief to those whom they thought deserving of help. A further clause in the act stated that if any individuals " do obstinately and frowardly refuse to give towards the help of the poor " they should be greatly exhorted by the vicar. If they still remained obstinate they were to be reported to the bishop, on whom lay the responsibility of sending for them " to induce and persuade him or them by charitable ways and means, and so according to his discretion to take order for the reformation thereof."

Thus, under pressure of social discontent, steps were being taken towards the evolution of a policy for dealing with the poor. So far the solution was not ideal, but it was something that the government had travelled thus far. The first signs of a recognition of the principle that the government had responsibilities in the problem of poverty had shown themselves, and progress along these lines was to be continued in the succeeding period until the full Tudor contribution to Poor Law

legislation had been achieved. The least en-
couraging contribution up to this point was that
made for the reduction of vagabondage. The
policy which sought to whip poverty out of England was a bankrupt one, for it showed that the
real meaning of that evil had not yet been grasped.
Only when it was recognized that economic disorganization, with its attendant evils of unemployment, sheer ill-luck, and genuine cases of
failure through no fault of the individual, were all
contributory factors which helped to swell the
army of vagabonds and able-bodied poor, only
then could a more enlightened policy be worked
out. That time had not come at the end of the
period with which this book is concerned. The
really constructive Poor Law is Elizabethan.

These were some of the problems to which
Tudor rule had given birth. They came to full
growth in the reign of the unfortunate Edward,
and they help materially to explain the difficulties
of the period. For these, combined with the
trials consequent upon the death of Henry VIII.
and the accession of a minor, form the key to the
reign. They were a combination of influences
which inevitably made the reign a difficult one,
and in face of the problem they present it will be
realized that the Tudor despotism, able to live on
through such conditions, was fixed on firm foundations. There is something to be said for an organization strong enough to prevent the return of the
chaos of the fifteenth century at a time when all
the elements for the making of such anarchy
seemed to be present.

CHAPTER X

INNOVATIONS IN RELIGION

IN December 1548 the reformer Peter Martyr wrote a letter from Oxford to his friend Martin Bucer at Strasburg. The student of the English Reformation should ponder some lines in that letter, for they will suggest to him the channel into which his thoughts should run if he would grasp what happened after Henry's death.

The writer, after announcing that the parliament was at work, goes on in the following words : " The other matter which distresses me not a little is this, that there is so much contention among our people about the Eucharist, that every corner is full of it. And even in the Supreme Council of the State, in which matters relating to religion are daily brought forward, there is so much disputing of the bishops among themselves, and with others, as I think was never heard before. Whence those who are in the Lower House, as it is called— that is, men of inferior rank—go up every day into the higher court of Parliament, not indeed for the purpose of voting (for that they do in the Lower House), but only that they may be able to hear these sharp and fervent disputations. Hitherto the popish party has been defeated, and the palm rests with our friends, but especially with the Archbishop of Canterbury, whom they till now were wont to traduce as a man ignorant of theology, and as being only conversant with matters of government; but now, believe me, he has shown himself so mighty a theologian against them as they would rather not have proof of, and they are compelled against their inclination to acknowledge his learning, and power and dexterity in debate. Transubstantiation, I think, is now exploded, and the difficulty respecting the Presence is at this time the most prominent point of dispute; but the parties engage with so much vehemence and energy as to occasion very great doubt as to the result, for the victory has hitherto been fluctuating between them. May the Holy Spirit grant that nothing may be determined upon but what may be for the advantage and welfare of the Church! With respect to a change of religion, they can no longer retrace their steps, for such great innovations have everywhere taken place, and all things are so changed and removed from their former state that if they were long suffered to remain so, wonderful disorder would ensue. Wherefore I have no doubt but that something must be decided upon; and I hope it may be under good auspices, and with the favour of Christ: and when this shall be the case, we must also entreat the Lord that the powers of hell, which are everywhere in arms, may not prevail against the truth of His word. . . ."

Into that letter he who knows may read the history of the religious changes taking place in the

Edwardian period. Let us see whither some of
the thoughts it suggests will lead us.

One thing is certain. They will lead us into
a new age. For if the political problems of the
reign of Edward VI. take us back to conditions
prevailing in the later Middle Ages, the religious
difficulties of the reign lead us just as surely into
the midst of a new world. The novelty of these
surroundings will not perplex those who have
studied with care the factors influencing Henry
VIII. in his work, but to those who forget that
there were other influences in action besides
politics to bring about the Reformation under
Henry, the change will seem so catastrophic
as to destroy the underlying continuity of the
history of those two reigns. It will hardly be
necessary to repeat at this stage the essential
problem Henry had tried to solve. What he had
been primarily concerned with was the supremacy
of State over Church. The goal he kept so clearly
in mind from beginning to end of his reign he may
be said to have reached, but the road by which
he walked towards it was strewn with many ruins.
It remained for those who followed him to clear
up the débris and begin to rebuild. The letter
quoted above suggests that they were soon engaged
on such work. For it will be noticed that the
interest of the new reign in the eyes of the letter-
writer was primarily theological. Henry's changes
had not, on the whole, meant much interference
with the doctrine of the Church in England ;
but the new relationships he had established made
some modifications of that doctrine inevitable,

and the reshaping had begun by the time Edward
VI. had been crowned king. Men were more
interested in debates on the Eucharist than in
statements of royal supremacy, transubstantiation
was not an academic question, but a matter
of practical politics, and a change in the form of
worship was an issue calling for the attention of
all those within the country who took an interest
in political and religious questions. In short, it
was the day of the theologian. The discussions
of bishops were of greater importance than the
activities of politicians. These were not the
questions that had absorbed men's attention in
the time of Henry VIII. They were the problems
of a new age.

There was, however, a link binding the old to
the new. The task of reconciling doctrine with
the changed religious conditions was largely
possible because of the work Henry VIII. had
done, for the new powers of the state made
easy the work of those bringing innovations in
doctrine, and the parliaments of the reign were
busy putting into statutory form decisions that
were to mould for generations the form of the
ritual of the English Church. From the point
of view of religion, then, Edward's reign does
not take its interest from any struggle for the
supremacy of the State over the Church. Such a
supremacy may from the beginning of the period
be taken for granted. What is really important
is the use to which these new powers of the State
were at last being put, and the nature of the beliefs
to be accepted as the standards for the Church

transcend in importance all questions about the relations between that institution and the crown.

The very fact that interest was centred on questions of doctrine meant that the whole nature of the English Reformation underwent a change. The new problems were not peculiarly English problems, and the evolution of creeds was a process visible elsewhere in Europe. England was at last drawn into the main stream of the controversies then raging over the continent, and the studied insularity of Henry's reformation movement could no longer be maintained. How great the change is suggested by Martyr's letter. Here was a foreigner in England, keenly interested in the religious controversies going on around him, and deeming them of sufficient importance to be described to a friend abroad. When we remember that Peter Martyr, a former Augustinian monk who had become a reformer and had fled from Germany after the Interim, was made professor of divinity at Oxford in 1549, we shall realize that he was not without influence in the country of his adoption. He was not the only reformer who had found England a safe refuge from the troubles of the continent. The chair of divinity at Cambridge was occupied by Martin Bucer, who had arrived from Germany in 1549 in the company of Fagius, a great Hebraist. John a Lasco, a Pole, had spent six months with Cranmer in 1548. In 1550 he returned from Friesland to make his home in England and to exercise an undoubted influence upon religious thought in this country. Pullain, or Vallerandus Pollanus, a minister at Strasburg,

came over with some of his flock after the Interim
and settled under the protection of Somerset at
Glastonbury. These were the most distinguished
of the reformers who had come to England.
They were not without considerable influence
upon the rapidly developing movement towards
reform. This foreign influence should suggest
what was happening. England had at last opened
its gates to the new theological learning, and the
spread of advanced religious ideas quickened with
the coming of the faithful.

This is not the place to open discussions about
the meaning of the religious changes transforming
the Europe of the sixteenth century, nor even to
attempt to sketch the direction in which such
changes went. All the same, if the English
Reformation is to be rightly understood, it is
necessary to bear in mind the reaction of the
continental Reformation movement upon the
religious thought of Englishmen. When Luther
published his *Theses* in 1519, he was not at all clear
as to the ultimate destination towards which he
was travelling, but the challenge he was making
was like a pebble thrown into the placid waters
of a pool. It woke to life ripples that were to go
on in ever-extending circles for generations, and
were to lead to results of which Luther and his
contemporaries could not have dreamed. Into a
world whose religious ideas were stereotyped he
had introduced some revolutionary principles. It
took some time for their real significance to be
grasped, and contemporaries who did not at first
catch his meaning cannot be blamed. Before them,

wherever they looked, they saw the Church their fathers had known. It was a Church with a world organization, the heir to the thoughts and the activities of all the ages, boasting an administrative organization that was all-embracing and firmly consolidated, in possession of creeds sealed by the authority of tradition. Orthodox Christianity rested on the Catholic Church : the Church had its foundations in the belief in the efficacy of the sacraments, and an insistence upon the divine office of the clergy. The duty of the ministers of the Church was that of conciliation between God and man. To a generation satisfied with such ideas Luther came as an iconoclast. His spiritual progress began with his idea of justification by faith, and controversy quickly forced him to base his arguments and his beliefs upon the ultimate authority of the scriptures. " Since your Majesty and your lordships ask for a plain answer, I will give you one without either horns or teeth," he said at Worms in 1521. " Unless I am convicted by Scripture, or by right reason (for I trust neither in popes nor in councils, since they have often erred and contradicted themselves)—unless I am thus convinced, I am bound by the texts of the Bible, my conscience is captive to the Word of God, I neither can nor will recant anything, since it is neither right nor safe to act against my conscience. God help me. Amen."

Not idly has it been said that Luther at Worms was the most pregnant and momentous fact in our history, though Luther did not know it as well as we do. For the ultimate result of the new idea was to be the liberation of conscience. The freedom of thought which had been permeating other spheres of human life in the renaissance period was at last entering into the religious life of man. The immediate results were rich in consequences. For the first implication of the new appeal to conscience was a challenge to the organization of the Church. Conscience took the place of the priest, and the clergy were faced by reformers who would rob them of their most important functions. This in itself was a vital division between the new and the old in religious thought, but there was a second result which was even more significant. It concerned the meaning of the newly-found idea of conscience. That Luther and the early reformers were clear as to the full meaning of this challenge to authority is more than doubtful, and the teaching they began to broadcast had not had time to grow before the new freedom degenerated into a licence which brought chaos. The new thought meant not unity but infinite division, not harmony but jangling discord. Instead of the simple beliefs of mediæval faith there were substituted the dogmas of a constantly increasing number of sects, and the quarrels of violently opposed schools of religious thought. Men were exercising their new-found right to individual interpretation of religious beliefs. The religious unity of the European world was shattered into a thousand fragments. Men waxed hot in disputes about doctrine and ritual.

Those conflicts reached England. The religious leaders of the reign of Edward VI. were in the very heart of the fray. In England, as elsewhere in Europe, there was being waged a grim conflict between two sets of religious ideas. Here, as elsewhere, it was the struggle of the old world against the new that was being fought out. On the one side were ranged those who found inspiration for their religious beliefs in the traditional theology symbolized in the Roman Church. On the other stood those who sought their inspiration in the scriptures. Those who wished to worship after the forms sanctioned by the immemorial traditions of the Church catholic were confronted by those who were seeking out a way of return to more primitive faiths. They thought they had found in the scriptures the basis for a simpler Christianity. To state the problem thus is to make it too simple. The leaders of the new thought were not more unanimous in England than they were abroad. The conflict was not a simple warfare between old ideas and new, for the new were in opposition to each other as well as to the old, and the problem of finding a *modus vivendi* looked as though it must remain for ever insoluble.

Those extreme zealots of the continental reform movement, who dreamed that a complete conquest of England by the new thought was a possibility, were to have a bitter hour of awakening. Even where all circumstances were favourable, and every influence available, the work done under Henry VIII. had been done sufficiently thoroughly to hinder a complete victory for the extreme in continental thought. The reforms of Edward's reign, advanced as they appear when they are contrasted with what had been accomplished previously, did not mean that there had been introduced into this country all the unadulterated ideas of the most extreme of continental schools. The point of real importance is that the European conflict was being waged in miniature. England had become one of the fronts in a far-flung battle-field. Little wonder that agents of the reform movement were active in propaganda work in this country, or that they watched with keen interest for news of the progress that was being made in the spread of new ideas in England. The bulky correspondence between reformers in England and their colleagues abroad—a large quantity of which has already been made available in print— is sufficient to show how strong that interest was. It is an eloquent testimony to the change which had come over the English Reformation movement. Between the Catholic and Protestant schools of thought—so violently opposed—there would seem to be little hope of compromise. And yet, it was to be the ultimate contribution of the religious leaders of the English Reformation movement to arrive at a solution of the problem that was unique. Such a result was largely possible because of the events which marked the reigns of Edward and Mary.

That spirit of compromise is foreshadowed in Peter Martyr's letter. It speaks of the increased prestige of the archbishop of Canterbury, and in thus introducing Thomas Cranmer to our notice, it provides us with a glimpse of an important figure in the religious life of Edward's reign. Martyr's words must not be taken to mean that in Cranmer the English Reformation movement found an heroic leader blazing fresh trails towards extreme Protestantism. Such an interpretation would miss the significance of Cranmer's work, and the methods by which reformation was furthered in the reign with which we are concerned. It must not be forgotten that throughout the reign of Edward the politicians were important figures. Somerset and Northumberland were both advocates of reform, but that they were so was due more to political than to religious reasons. In Somerset's case, it is true, some element of genuine religious conviction may fairly be credited as a motive force behind his policy ; but in Northumberland's character there was little to suggest that even the baser motives of the reformers were low enough to provide him with an incentive for reform. He was an opportunist gambling for a higher stake than the establishment of creeds, and he clutched at the support of one party in the religious controversy because he believed it would enable him to achieve his own ignoble ambitions. Whatever their motives, the political leaders had their parts to play in the religious history of the reign. Partly through conviction, and partly because they saw in the radical party a support for their own plans, both Somerset and Northumberland were ready to inaugurate change within the Church. Their methods were not similar. Under Protector

Somerset the advance in the direction of reform was definite enough, but it was steady and, on the whole, slow. Under Northumberland the desperate gamble in political adventures was accompanied by a similar wild rush in the direction of extreme reform, and the caution characteristic of the first phase was thrown to the winds. Closer study will show that neither these men nor the policies they represent are the real topic of interest in the religious history of this period. Behind them stands Thomas Cranmer. He presents something of a problem, because his life-work was so paradoxical. He profoundly influenced the movement towards reform, because he lacked the personality to come forward as a powerful leader. The source of his strength lay always in his weakness. His was the temperament attracted by compromise, and in his efforts to achieve it will be found the true significance of the part he played in the Edwardian reforms.

During the reign of Henry VIII. Cranmer's intellectual development had been steady, and the progress he made was in the direction of the "new learning" in theology. Even in the later years of the reign Cranmer, who had done so much to suggest to Henry the policy which marked the crucial years of the Reformation, was still in possession of his master's support. He had need of it, for in the later phase, when the Catholic reaction, typified in Stephen Gardiner, bishop of Winchester, was making a desperate fight for control of policy, there were not wanting serious efforts to deprive him of royal favour. Henry

VIII., however, remained attached to him until the end, and Cranmer was one of the few men who had no reason to complain of Henry's faithlessness. His good fortune had a direct bearing on the course of the Reformation. Henry's support gave Cranmer the leisure and the peace which enabled him to continue his theological studies, and he was thus able to prepare himself for the work which fell to his lot in the next reign. The fruits of his labours were being seen as early as 1545, when his Litany was given to the world. Its importance is not primarily theological, for the ideas it contained were in large measure borrowed from the old. But the new Litany showed that a master of English prose was at work, and in the beautiful phrasing of this work Cranmer bequeathed to the English Church a form of service which was to remain almost unchanged until modern times, and which would keep bright the memory of its author long after many of his less attractive qualities had been forgotten. The Litany was not by any means the whole of Cranmer's work. The results of this period of contemplation were yet to be carried into practice, and by the beginning of Edward's reign Cranmer was ready to take up his task. His contact with the leaders of continental religious thought supplied him with inspiration and ideas. It would be a mistake to think of him as an original thinker who saw crystal clear before him the solution of the religious difficulties of his day. He was easily influenced by any mind stronger than his own with which he came in contact. Thus his progress was uncertain, for he was attracted by ideas gleaned from the various sects then active in Europe. Neither Lutherans nor Zwinglians could claim him for themselves, and the ultimate beliefs at which he arrived contained much that was not the monopoly of any one school of thought. The limitations of his own mind affected his own religious beliefs, and thus directly influenced the course of the Reformation in England. Throughout his life Cranmer's weakness was his eagerness for compromise. He would have been a more attractive figure in the history of his times had he been strong enough to make a more determined stand on one side or the other, but it is possible to imagine that such heroic action would have had less important results than those which followed from his weakness. Cranmer believed that he had found the secret for the solution of the religious difficulties around him in compromise, and his efforts to find a *via media* in matters of faith and ritual influenced all the religious history of the Edwardian period. Here lies the secret of Cranmer's importance, and those who seek to understand the religious history of Edward's reign will do well to remember that behind the activity of the political leaders of the Reformation there was going on the steady development of the theological ideas of Thomas Cranmer, which found expression in forms of service that were literature as well as theology.

Somerset's protectorate opened with an administrative action which foreshadowed the policy to be adopted during his tenure of office. In 1547

England was divided into six circuits, and commissioners were appointed, comprising clergy and laymen, who were to visit the chief churches of the districts. They took with them Injunctions modelled on those issued in 1536 and 1538 for the regulation of Church services; but the new Injunctions were more complete than those which had preceded them, and they must be read as an indication of a further advance in the direction of reform which was now contemplated. They gave directions for preaching which urged attacks upon Roman Catholic and superstitious usages within the Church. In this they were, of course, following the earlier precedents, but they went further. While the confessional and prayers for the dead were retained, war was declared against superstition, and orders were given for the abolition of shrines, the use of candlesticks, images, and pictures within churches. More definitely indicative of the tendency towards advance was the stress laid upon the use of the Bible. The clergy were ordered to read and teach the scriptures, and in addition they were to use the Paraphrases of Erasmus, while special emphasis was laid upon the use of the English language in Church services. Further, instructions were issued for reading the Book of Homilies, regulations were made for clerical education, Sunday observance, the ceremonies that were to be retained, and the discipline that was to govern the lives of the clergy. The Injunctions were ordered to be read once every quarter in church. Thus, while the new Injunctions were decidedly

223

moderate, and did little more than enforce the policy which had been the ideal of Henry VIII. and Cromwell, they were an unmistakable sign that more was yet to come, and they showed that the government soon proposed to take the Church a little farther on the road towards reform than Henry VIII. had done. The immediate future saw such a policy initiated.

In 1547 parliament met, and legislation on religious matters came up for discussion. By the Statute of Treasons the heresy laws and the Act of Six Articles of the previous reign were repealed, and reformed thought was thus given an opportunity to spread in the country. The preamble to that act is eloquent of the changed attitude of the government towards the religious problem. It reads as follows : " Nothing being more godly, more sure, more to be wished and desired, betwixt a Prince, the Supreme Head and Ruler, and the subjects whose governor and head he is than on the Prince's part great clemency and indulgency, and rather too much forgiveness and remission of his royal power and just punishment than exact severity and justice to be shewed, and on the subjects' behalf that they should obey rather for love, and for the necessity and love of a king and prince than for fear of his strait and severe laws ; yet such time cometh in the commonwealth that it is necessary and expedient for the repressing of the insolency and unruliness of men, and for the foreseeing and providing of remedies against rebellion. . . . The which thing caused the Prince of most famous memory, King

Henry the Eighth . . . to make and enact certain laws and statutes which might seem and appear . . . very extreme and terrible. . . . But, as in tempest or winter one course and garment is convenient, in calm or warm weather a more liberal race or lighter garment both may and ought to be followed and used, so we have seen divers strait and sore laws made in one Parliament, the time so requiring, in a more calm and quiet reign of another Prince, by like authority and Parliament repealed and taken away." And then follow the clauses which do away with the " winter garments " of Henry's reign, that legislation which had been designed to put a curb on too rapid a growth of radical ideas.

This legislation was followed by an act for the election of bishops, which was in the traditional line of policy of the last reign. It changed the method of creating bishops by substituting a form of appointment through royal letters patent for the older form of a *congé d'elire*. This completed the work of the former reign in the interests of the state. The higher clergy now became little better than civil servants. Finally, the work of this parliament included an act which brought to its logical conclusion the policy of spoliation of the Church.

By the dissolution of the chantries and kindred institutions which encouraged " vain opinion of purgatory," a fresh step in secularization was completed. The chantries may be defined roughly as endowed chapels with special priests whose function it was to say masses for the souls of the founders of the chantries. But the act cast a wider net. Not merely chantries, but all gilds, fraternities, or colleges whose funds were in part or wholly devoted to such superstitious purposes were to be deprived of all such funds. It was the last act in the policy for which Henry VIII. and Cromwell must be condemned. The significance of this piece of legislation has been summed up in quaint language. It was " the last dish of the last course : after chantries, as after cheese, nothing is to be expected." Like much of the legislation of the Reformation, the Chantries Act has a theory behind it which makes it possible to work out a superficial justification, at any rate, for what was done ; but the argument is fragile. The avowed object of the confiscation was stated to be the endowment of education. Further, the spoliation was not to be carried out without some compensation for those priests who were thus dispossessed. Provision was also to be made for carrying on the educational work of those gilds and colleges which had performed such duties. So far so good. Unfortunately, as in the case of the monasteries in the previous reign, so now, pious aspirations remained pious aspirations. The few grammar schools founded were not enough to make up for the educational facilities lost. The truth is that Edward VI.'s reputation as an educationalist is undeserved, for the schools which bear his name were not of his foundation. His only credit must be that he spared some of the foundations made long before his time. The act was, in fact, mere spoliation. It is for that reason to be condemned.

It was probably less hypocritical in intention than it proved to be in practice, but it was beyond the power of its framers to devise an adequate means of giving effect to their schemes. The ultimate history of the sequestration follows that of the legislation concerning the monasteries. Most of the proceeds was squandered on place hunters, and the state gained little or nothing from the transaction.

Important as such legislation was, it had as yet done little more than open the way for licence and the encouragement of advanced thought. It was not long before the need for legislation of a disciplinary character was realized. The liberty of the first years rendered the service of the English Church chaotic, and an attempt had to be made to introduce order. That attempt was made in the Book of Common Prayer, and the first Act of Uniformity for the enforcement of its use was passed in 1549. It was concerned with the form of the Church service, not with theological disputes, and its object was the enforcement of one form of service throughout the country. Like the rest of the measures of the first phase of the reign, it was cautious reform. It has been sometimes regarded as influenced by Lutheran ideas, but as one historian has pointed out, this was due " not so much to conscious imitation as to the common conservatism which characterized the Lutheran and Anglican service books and led to the retention in them of many Catholic usages which Reformed churches in Europe rejected."

One more act of this first phase calls for mention. In 1549 a statute gave force to the principle which Convocation had discussed and agreed to as early as 1547. The ideal of celibacy of the clergy was now recognized as one not easily achieved, and permission was granted for the clergy to marry. With that act the work of the first phase was complete. On the whole, what had been done so far was moderate. The changes made were cautious in conception and realization, so that it would be wrong to describe the legislation as favourable to the ideas of the extreme reformers in England. The pace at which the Reformation moved in the second phase was, on the other hand, much more rapid. Under the Northumberland régime the policy of caution was rejected, and it looked as though the party of extreme reform was on the point of fastening its opinions on the nation so securely that they would not be easily removed.

This second phase opened in 1550 with legislation that was a fitting prelude to such a policy. In order to leave no excuse for breaches of uniformity as it had been sanctioned for church worship, another statute was passed ordering the destruction of all service books other than that prescribed by law. Another gave the government power to appoint a commission for the reform of the canon law—a reform rendered very necessary after the events of the last reign ; while yet another gave similar powers for the appointment of a commission to draw up an Ordinal. Such legislation was only a prelude. The new phase was soon marked by definitely aggressive action against Catholics. The members of the council who still adhered to the old religion were expelled, and the executive—packed in Northumberland's interests —sank to a state of corruption rarely seen in English history. By means of it Northumberland maintained his grip upon the country, and he resisted successfully all efforts to call a parliament which he feared would be—as an inevitable result of the hatred which his policy was arousing— favourable to his rival Somerset.

Meanwhile great religious changes were made. In March 1550 a new Ordinal was adopted which swept away much Catholic ritual from religious services. More definite advance was that symbolized in the second Act of Uniformity of 1552, the object of which was to enforce the use of a revised Prayer Book. The new book, primarily the work of Cranmer, but influenced also by the ideas of his foreign friends Peter Martyr and Bucer, was an advance on the first. It showed a move in the direction of advanced continental thought, though at the same time it displayed signs of the insular quality of English religious ideas. It was not advanced enough for the extremists, and it cannot be regarded as an imitation of any particular continental school of thought. The Act of Uniformity which was to enforce its use was severe. Abstention from church on Sundays and holy days was to be punished by ecclesiastical censure and excommunication. More severe punishment was reserved for deliberate breaches of the new settlement. Attendance at service where forms other than those of the new Prayer Book were used was to be punished by six months' imprisonment. If the offence was repeated, the punishment was to be doubled, and for a third offence the penalty was to be life imprisonment.

One more of Cranmer's activities deserves notice before the history of the religious changes of this period is lost in the heavy atmosphere surrounding Northumberland's last gamble for power. The man who had striven hard to reform the English Church without committing it irrevocably to the fanatical schemes of radical reformers, aimed at solving all difficulties by evolving a creed for Englishmen. To this end he had worked for some years before he brought his articles forward in 1551 for the criticism of the bishops. After much discussion and amendment they were accepted, and by May 1553 they were being enforced. It was Cranmer's fond belief that he had at last settled English problems. After these articles had been subscribed by the clergy he thought " that such a concord and quietness in religion shall shortly follow thereof, as else is not to be looked for many years." It is amazing to think he could have dreamed of such a possibility, for there were at that time in England at least three parties which were poles asunder in their ideas and schemes. There was, in the first place, the party of extremist reformers working under the direction of continental influences and stimulated by the progress already made. Their object was to introduce into England the movement already proving so successful in Switzerland. There was, at the opposite extreme, a party who loathed all the work of reformation carried out under Henry VIII. and Edward. Their sympathy was with Rome, and though they were not numerically strong, they were a powerful influence on behalf of Rome. And finally, between these two extremes there was a party of compromise. Their support was given to all which had happened up to the promulgation of the First Book of Common Prayer, but beyond this they were not prepared to go. To bring together into a single Church such violently opposed groups was an impossibility, and Cranmer's attempt proved to be as complete a failure as might have been expected.

The story of the last few months of Edward's reign belongs in the main to political narrative ; but the failure of Northumberland's schemes reacted very thoroughly upon religious history. When his plans for securing the crown for Lady Jane Grey were wrecked, the downfall of the reform party was also assured. It would be a mistake to attribute this failure, and the events subsequent to it, to a genuine love of Roman Catholicism on the part of the majority of Englishmen. The reaction towards Rome came less from religious fervour than from a deep desire for political security, and a profound weariness with the corrupt rule of Northumberland. All the same, whatever be the reason to which it must be ascribed, the reaction was sure. It involved a course of events which make a new chapter in the history of Tudor England.

CHAPTER XI

THE reign of Mary Tudor once came into the view of a critic, who thought he had said all there was to be said about it when he had summed it up as "a parenthesis in the Tudor period." Since then it has become impossible to consider the reign without using that phrase, and we must pay lip service, at any rate, to historical fashions. Once this has been done, it must be insisted that the point of view this phrase suggests is a poor one from which to look at the reign, and the criticism implicit in it does much less than justice to the years from 1553 to 1558. For this epigram may mean at least two things, and neither is entirely true. In the first place, it may be construed as a suggestion that the years from 1553 to 1558 can be removed from the history of the Tudor period without affecting the general development, in much the same way as a parenthetical clause may be omitted from a sentence without altering its general sense. Or, in the second place, it may be used to imply that Mary's reign is so different in character from the other reigns of the Tudor period that it cannot be summed up with them, though some similarities make it impossible

232

to omit it entirely from the general survey, so that it has to be mentioned in a parenthetical clause suggesting its connection with, and difference from, the others. Neither of these suggestions is a reliable clue to the reign, though each suggests much that is true ; and it would be hard to find a better way of dealing with the period than that which seeks to probe the truth and falsity of each of these assumptions.

Suppose we start with the hypothesis that Mary's reign is unimportant in the Tudor period, that what happened during the years when she was in power can be omitted without materially altering the general tendency of English development in the sixteenth century. Such an opinion can only be arrived at by deliberately ignoring much that went on during the reign, and it leads to an under-emphasis—even to a neglect—of factors whose influence was not confined to the years 1553–58. The advocates of such a view are the first to concentrate their attention upon the importance of the Elizabethan period. In the work done by that great queen, they see the full achievement of Tudor policy. They look upon Elizabeth's reign as the splendid conclusion of Tudor history. They are entitled to such an opinion, but it is worth pointing out to them that they will not in the least belittle Elizabeth's work if they recognize the vital truth that without the reign of Mary that of her successor becomes well-nigh unintelligible. Most of the problems with which Elizabeth had to deal owed their peculiar nature to events in the reign of Mary. Many of

233

them, indeed, owed their very existence to that period. The Church settlement at which Elizabeth was to arrive could never have been reached had it not been for the consequences of Mary's religious policy. The Spanish problem, looming so large in Elizabethan politics, could never have arisen in the special form in which it did had it not been for the special relationship between Spain and England which was the direct result of Mary's own work. The contacts between Elizabeth and her parliaments, indeed her relationship with the country in general, were to no small extent the result of lessons learned by Mary's mistakes. Even Elizabeth's own position on the throne was not unaffected by the ideas which had been developed after the accession of Mary. Thus, from the standpoint of Elizabeth's reign it is clear that the reign of her predecessor was all-important, and any attempt at understanding the final phase of Tudor history must start by a comprehensive survey of the reign of Mary.

In the same way, a full understanding of the peculiar contribution of the sixteenth century to English history calls for a study of Mary's reign. The Tudor despotism is not completely intelligible without an examination of the reign of Mary, for those years provided a remarkable commentary on the system. They showed, in the first place, what that machinery of government could do. Mary achieved a great deal during her life, and much of what she did she would not have been able to accomplish without the aid of the system Henry VII. and Henry VIII. had established. But Mary did not succeed in doing all that she would have liked to do. That, too, was due to the Tudor despotism. She was to find that the system we are sometimes tempted to regard as omnicompetent had its limitations. They are not easily seen in the reign of Henry VIII., nor are they altogether clear in the reign of Elizabeth. It is to Mary's reign that we must go if we seek the full indication of the limitations of the Tudor despotism. Lastly, her reign was in many ways the climax of problems that had been growing throughout the early Tudor period. Questions that had been begging for answers for years were at last dealt with, and the conflict of ideas had results which reacted with some consequence on the future history of England.

Nor was Mary's reign so entirely devoid of permanent results as is sometimes supposed. Sterility, it has been said, is the keynote to the reign, and on the first glance it would appear a negligible period in our history, since much of what Mary did was to be immediately undone by her successor. On a wider view it will be seen that these generalizations need some qualification. The facts of history cannot be wiped out as though they were scribblings on a slate which can be entirely removed with a damp duster. They leave traces behind them that can never be completely forgotten. It was possible to repeal Marian legislation, but the policy of which that legislation was but an outward sign had indirect effects whose influence was permanent. Decisions were taken, policy was worked out, which could never be undone, and the result was that, although at first sight it looks as though Elizabeth's reign was a reaction from that of Mary, events made it impossible for that reaction to swing England back to a position occupied before Mary's reign. When Elizabeth began her work she could not act as though Mary had never lived.

So much, then, for the idea that Mary's reign was of little or no consequence, that it may be passed over as a parenthetic clause in the story of Tudor history. What can be said about the more reasonable interpretation, which would dismiss the acts of the reign as a negation of Tudor policy, and the period as one to be dealt with separately as an exception that proves the generalizations to be made on Tudor rule ?

It is possible to collect attractive speculations which seem to suggest the truth of this opinion. In Mary, half a Spaniard as she was, there came into the Tudor period a monarch out of touch with her subjects, and unable to understand their views. Thus the queen failed from the very beginning to hold popular sympathy. Never, at any moment, was she able to achieve the most characteristic of Tudor accomplishments. She could not put her finger on the national pulse. She was never able to become what the other Tudors were able to become almost instinctively. She never appeared as the symbol of the nation. On the contrary, the whole of her life-work marked her out as anti-English. She seemed to her subjects incapable of appreciating at their true value the powers and privileges of kingship. Men who knew how high had been the price at which the new monarchy had been bought were not easily propitiated when they saw it thrown away in the interests of Spain or Rome. They could not respect a monarch who failed to keep in her own hands all the power Henry VIII. had acquired by his life-work. Thus Mary seemed to contemporaries a dangerous ruler, because she did not work for what they had been brought up to believe were Tudor ideals. She was different from her father, and men realized with misgiving how some of the ideas he had spent all his energies in translating into action were not only unintelligible to Mary, but were actually destroyed by her policy. Such thoughts as these suggest that there is truth in the view of Mary as a monarch utterly alien to the spirit of the Tudor monarchy.

It is only half the truth. There were features of Mary's reign most strongly suggestive of characteristics to be recognized as essentially Tudor in quality. The problems of the reign were predominantly Tudor in nature. Like Henry VIII. before her, and Elizabeth after, Mary was to find most of her difficulties grow out of a problem monotonously familiar to those who have followed thus far the fortunes of her house. It was the old problem of the royal marriage which was to cause most of her difficulties. Like her father, Mary made a mistake in her marriage. As in his case, so in hers, the marriage question was to be one which affected Anglo-Spanish relations, and the domestic and foreign politics of England were to be influenced by considerations which were to be found in the policy of Spain. That was not all. The marriage policy was linked to another familiar problem. Just as in other Tudor reigns the closely allied question of the succession to the throne was a dominant issue in politics, so the succession problem played its part in Mary's reign. Henry VIII. had dared much in the desperate gamble for a solution of the succession problem. Elizabeth was to juggle with the problem throughout her reign. Mary lived through years of sorrow, praying for the heir that fate refused.

Nor was Mary altogether anti-Tudor either in the ideals of her policy or in the methods whereby she tried to achieve them. To her people she was fated to appear as one who thought little of England. In reality it was her love for her people which made her do much that she did. She honestly believed that, however great the success of her predecessors, all their victories sank into insignificance beside the tremendous fact that they had put the souls of their subjects in deadly peril of damnation. For Mary's attention was concentrated on the task of saving her people from the wrath to come reserved for the schismatic. She felt that all she did was justified because of the greatness of the issues at stake. According to her light she was as ardently patriotic as any of the Tudors, and the honesty of her motives gives a touch of authenticity to the legendary forecast that upon her death Calais would be found written upon her heart. In all she did she thought she was acting in the best interests of her country. Not all her work is to be condemned. She shouldered responsibility for the debts of Henry VIII. and Edward VI. She tried to undo some of the evils of her predecessors by issuing new coinage to replace the debased issue. She planned an economy campaign, and lessened the burdens of taxation. The general lines of her policy— anti-English as they seemed to contemporaries— were the result of a genuine attempt to achieve what Mary believed to be the best interests of England. Thus her policy, misguided as it must appear, was not without some flavour of the Tudor spirit, and the methods whereby she sought to achieve it were even more reminiscent of the family to which she belonged. In her methods there was the same fixed purpose which characterized and explains much of the success of the Tudors. Like the rest of them, she kept constantly in mind the objective at which she aimed. There was, too, the same ruthlessness. Knowing what she wanted, she was determined to win it, and the will of the sovereign crushed in true Tudor fashion those individuals who sought to prevent the attainment of royal ideals. She even went so far as to try to use the most characteristic of all Tudor methods. She employed parliament to give her policy all the force of authority. In many ways the most instructive feature of her reign is the way in which the sovereignty of Henry VIII. was utilized to work out a royal policy that would have horrified that monarch. It was the supreme state which was in action, and the will of the sovereign was being enforced upon the country in precisely the same way as the royal will of Henry VIII. had been. Marian policy differed from that of Henry, but the difference was in some ways less arresting than the similarity. For Mary, like her father, believed her own ideas were those best suited to the national needs, and she held as strongly as Henry had done that what she did was right. The similarities between Henry and Mary must not be pressed too far. There was a fundamental difference between them and the policies they sought to introduce, but the differences are such as are best understood by a more detailed examination of Mary's work.

Thus there were as many Tudor qualities in the reign of Mary as there were features the reverse of those the word Tudor brings to the mind. No epigram which only stresses the un-Tudor characteristics is a sufficient clue to the period. It will at best express only half the truth. Where, then, does the significance of Mary Tudor's reign lie ?

Two, at least, of the movements which go to make the history of those years call for some mention in any answer to that question. They justify the view that the policy of the period was important, and they go to prove that the continuity conspicuous in Tudor history as a whole is not completely broken by this phase, for they are themselves movements which had run through the earlier years and continued to be of importance until the sixteenth century ran to its close. The first of them is the familiar religious movement. The second is a political movement. In the Marian attempt to solve the Reformation puzzle and in the marriage alliance with Spain will be found the key problems of the reign.

The reign of Mary was to show that what had been happening to the Church in England since 1529 was not to go unchallenged. From the beginning she stood out as the leader of the English Counter-reformation, and her reign is the story of a desperate conflict. She was the symbol of militant Catholicism, and there is something not altogether unattractive in the picture of her as the zealous leader of a lost cause. What happened under her leadership was war. Although she was destined to be found fighting for a losing cause, it was one which did not go down without a struggle, and in the struggle wounds were inflicted on the victors which would cripple them in future years. In a word, Mary's challenge had an important result, for it meant that the religious situation could never again be what it had been under Edward VI. By checking the headlong movement in the direction of extreme reform Mary made it inevitable that the ultimate settlement of Church affairs in England should be different from what would have been the case if she had never reigned. It was Mary's peculiar contribution that made possible a solution of religious difficulties in a way unique in Europe. Under Elizabeth a settlement was made of which it could later be said that this country " was not Catholic, as countries which accepted the decrees of the Council of Trent understood Catholicism : still less was she Protestant, as Calvin and William the Silent understood Protestantism." That English compromise can only be interpreted through the work of Mary.

In a similar way, Mary's contribution to political history was not altogether uncreative. To her lot fell the task of wakening national emotions which before her time were hardly fully grown. Her misguided Spanish policy was vital. It brought home to English minds, as nothing else could possibly have done, the meaning of the most ominous movement in the whole of sixteenth-century history. England awoke to the possibilities implicit in Spanish imperialism. If, during her reign, there was going on in England a life and death struggle between the old and new within the Church, there was also being prepared an equally deadly conflict between Spain and England. Either of these movements would be sufficient to impart an interest to the years under examination. Taken together, they make a study of them indispensable.

Religion was the motive force of Mary's life-work. It will, therefore, be a fitting prelude to a closer study of her reign to attempt a sketch of the aims and methods of her ecclesiastical policy. There was nothing complicated about either of them. The daughter of Henry VIII. and Catherine could hardly be expected to cherish tolerance towards the consequences which had flowed from Henry's repudiation of her mother. Her early training had taught her to hate the word reform and everything connected with it. Throughout the reign of her father—and of her brother—she had suffered indignities which left an indelible mark on her mind and character, but she continued faithful to her mother's cause despite all the pressure put upon her to desert it. When her chance came, and she was queen in England, she was determined to blot out the ugly past and restore the state of things which had existed in the happier days before the Reformation Parliament had worked the will of Henry VIII. on Church and State. She had the wit to see the difficulties in her path, and her policy was set in order to avoid them. It fell, therefore, into two phases. In the first of them—which ran from 1553 to 1554—she was content with the rejection of the religious reforms of Edward's reign, so that her work went no farther than the establishment of the *status quo* of the latter years of Henry VIII. But in the second phase—which continued from 1554 until 1558—she had more ambitious aims. She dreamed of realizing the complete reconciliation of England and Rome by the utter defeat of the Reformation movement in this country. She made a desperate effort to achieve her end, but she had taken up an impossible task, and ultimately she was bound to fail. In the first phase of her policy she worked mainly through Stephen Gardiner, bishop of Winchester, whose ideals, generally speaking, were those of the Henrician settlement. In the later phase she was under the domination of cardinal Pole, who was the incarnation of papal ideals. In the first phase she worked her will by means of the royal supremacy and by the assent of parliament. In the second,

243

she acted more autocratically. She restored Catholicism, and the Roman Church again ruled in England.

Her first parliament gave her the first Statute of Repeal in 1553. This made a clean sweep of Edwardian religious legislation. Statutes of the previous reign dealing with the sacrament of the altar, the election of bishops, the first Act of Uniformity, the marriage of priests, the use of images, the second Act of Uniformity, the keeping of holy days, were all repealed. The new situation was described in the act itself, which stated that " all such divine services and administration of sacraments as were most commonly used in the realm of England in the last years of the reign of our late sovereign lord King Henry the Eighth, shall be, from and after the 20th day of December (1553), used and frequented throughout the whole realm of England." It was followed by Injunctions issued to the bishops in March 1554. They were ordered to restore the old forms, prevent heretics from being appointed to benefices, punish those who spread false doctrines, and remove married priests. In effect, what they aimed at and what they achieved was a return to the religious settlement of Henry VIII.

It was something to have undone all the work of Edward's reign, but more was to come. If a stand is taken somewhere about January 1555 it is possible to obtain a good view of these changes. By that date important steps had been taken. In the first place, the marriage of Mary and Philip of Spain, on which the queen had set her heart—and about which more will be heard in the later years of the reign—had become an accomplished fact. Philip had landed in England on July 20, 1554, and had been married to Mary on 25th July at Winchester Cathedral. In the second place, something had occurred that would have appeared utterly improbable to contemporaries if they had been told of it a few years earlier. Accustomed as they were to miraculous changes, which in a twinkling of an eye could transform the world in which they lived, they would have needed imaginative gifts of a high order to have enabled them to foretell that on November 24, 1554, a cardinal of the Roman Church, with his silver cross carried in state before him, would arrive in London and be received in full ceremony by the queen. Reginald Pole, cardinal and *legatus a latere*, had come home from his exile. The proud descendant of royalty, the enemy of Henry VIII. and all his works, the servant whose life had been consecrated to the service of the Church for which his love was a passion, had returned to reconcile his countrymen to Rome. The miracle which had occurred will not be explained by a study of Pole. His zeal could not have achieved such success. There was a third factor that must be called into account. Pole would not have been in England if the parliament which met in November 1554 had not acquiesced. On 29th November that assembly passed a petition praying for reunion with Rome. On the 30th November the king and queen assembled with the parliament at Whitehall,

245

interceded on behalf of their country, and cardinal Pole pronounced the realm absolved from schism. The reconciliation was accomplished. It was quickly followed by legislation, and by January 1555 parliament had passed several important acts. By one, which the previous parliament had refused, it restored the heresy laws of Richard II., Henry IV., and Henry V. It passed a second Repeal Act, couched in most humble language, stating that the country " had swerved from the obedience of the See Apostolic, and declined from the unity of Christ's Church " until such times as it seemed good to God to send cardinal Pole, *legatus a latere*, " to call us home again into the right way from whence we have all this long while wandered and strayed abroad." All of which was the prodigal's prelude to a rescinding of all the acts passed against Rome since the year 1528 . . . with some exceptions whose significance must not be slurred over without notice.

On the surface it would appear that the great work had been done, and that England was again in harmony with Rome. Appearances are often deceptive. What remains to be said makes it doubtful whether these proceedings can be regarded as a change of heart. For throughout the negotiations that led to the result just mentioned one important question had been kept constantly to the front. Before Pole was allowed to return he was expressly told that he would have to receive back into the fold of the Catholic Church the men who had been concerned in the breach. He must give them absolution for their sins, but he must not expect the restitution of any of the wealth of the Church that had been sequestrated. The second Act of Repeal, which showed the return of the penitents into the bosom of the Church, went on to discuss in a very practical manner the question of the retention of ecclesiastical property by those who held it at the time. It stated the principle that " all such causes and quarrels as by pretence of the said schism, or by any other jurisdiction ecclesiastical whatsoever, might be moved, by the Pope's Holiness or See Apostolic, or by any other jurisdiction ecclesiastical, may be utterly removed and taken away : so as all persons having sufficient conveyance of the said lands and hereditaments, goods, and chattels, as is aforesaid by the common laws, acts, or statutes of this realm, may without scruple of conscience enjoy them, without impeachment or trouble by pretence of any General Council, canons, or ecclesiastical law, and clear from all dangers of the canons of the Church." The sinners were repenting, but they had no intention of giving up the profits of their sins.

Here we touch upon the most significant issue in the Marian religious settlement. It should be studied, because it suggests at least two conclusions which shed considerable light upon Reformation history. For, in the first place, this conditional reconciliation is a striking illustration of what Henry VIII. achieved when he linked up his Reformation settlement with the spoliation of the Church. And, in the second place, it proves that in the Marian conflict between the old and

247

the new the Church of Rome had definitely lost. The Henrician policy had pandered to the selfish desires of a land-hungry party, and it had thereby made certain that never again would the Church of Rome exercise in England all the powers and privileges it had once enjoyed.

There was, however, one crucial problem which still remained unsolved. The restoration of a *status quo* could not give back to the Church the possessions which had been lost. A large proportion of its wealth was irretrievably gone. But the reconciliation did give back possession of many ecclesiastical privileges. This was no small gift, and it might have meant the beginnings of a more complete victory for the Church had it been properly exploited. The final condemnation of Roman policy in England in the days of success under Mary must be that it tried to do too much, and did it too hurriedly. Stimulated by the fanatical zeal of Mary, a policy of persecution was decided upon, and ecclesiastical jurisdiction was used to provide material for bonfires. The story is a melancholy one, and to embark upon a minute examination of the persecution which stained the later years of the reign from 1555 until the end, would be to illustrate by innumerable examples how great an attempt was being made to frighten reformers and their beliefs out of England. Although the narrative must be omitted in detail, it would be wrong to pass without mention of three cases whose importance lay in the influence their victims exercised upon public opinion. In October 1555 Latimer and Ridley were burned at Oxford. They were followed later by Cranmer. The archbishop had been arrested in September 1553, but it was not easy to deal with him owing to his position. It was not until September 1555 that his trial was concluded, and on December 4, 1555, he was deprived of his archbishopric and handed over to the secular power. On March 21, 1556, he, too, was burned at Oxford.

As long as men study this period there will always be divers opinions of Cranmer's character, but there can be no quarrel with an estimate attributing to him a leading place in the story of the English Reformation. To a greater extent than any other man he influenced the direction in which that movement was to run. Yet the tragedy of his career lies in his helplessness before the forces he was in part responsible for developing. It was not for lack of learning, nor for want of a religious faith, that he died. The shadow on his path was that which darkened every man's career in those troubled times. It was the reconciliation of the interests of Church and State which perplexed his mind, as it did the mind of every leader of his generation. Henry VIII. had reopened an age-old problem in a new form, and Cranmer could no more solve that problem than could any others amongst his contemporaries. Hence the servile obedience to Henry VIII. so often interpreted as the sign of a cowardly place-hunter. Hence the efforts at compromise so easily misread as indications of weak-mindedness. Hence, too, the recantations marking his last days.

Cranmer cannot be explained by his biography. He has to be studied through the details of the Tudor period. He was what his age had made him, and in the multifarious movements crossing and recrossing those troubled years will be found the clue to a personality who stands out as a leader —albeit an undecided one—in his generation. Latimer, Ridley, Cranmer—these three were outstanding names, but it must be remembered that they were only the greatest among many. The estimate that makes the burnings of those years total something like three hundred is probably no exaggeration.

The significance of the policy of persecution is psychological. " Be of good comfort," said the aged Latimer to Ridley, " we shall this day light a candle, by God's grace, in England, as I trust shall never be put out." Latimer died a prophet as well as a martyr. The effect of the burnings was undeniable. They sealed once for all the fate of the Church militant, and the partial defeat symbolized by the retention of Church lands was turned into a complete disaster by the burnings. The reign of Mary reveals the lost cause making its last fight, but it brings out clearly, as well, the greatness of the opportunity that was being thrown away. Persecution on the scale then practised horrified English opinion, and upon Mary and the leaders of the Church must be fixed the responsibility for the fierce antagonism that was in future to flourish in England against the Church of Rome. Here, then, lies the ultimate importance of Mary's religious policy. Her reign, and only her reign, can explain why it was that a return to a *status quo* was impossible. That is why her policy needs careful attention as an essential prelude to the study of religious history in England in the reign of her successor.

Important as the period was when judged from the standpoint of religion, it was no less important from a more political point of view. For just as in religious history the reign saw a gradual revulsion from Rome, so in political history its main significance lies in the steadily growing antipathy towards Spain. It was a feeling that flourished upon Mary's mistakes. She ascended the throne in circumstances which made such unpopularity as she excited unlikely. She had no one to blame save herself for the change that was sure to appear. For she began with demonstrations of public support which made her the occupant of what appeared to be the most safely planted of all Tudor thrones. She was the symbol of the happy far-off days before Anne Boleyn. About her birth— whatever legal fictions had to say on the matter— there was in fact no shadow of stain. She was the lawful issue of a marriage that the English people in heart had never renounced, and her tragic childhood won her the sympathy of her subjects. The desperate gamble of Northumberland had, moreover, strengthened the bonds between her and them. It was a support that was eloquent testimony of the benefits of Tudor rule. For the menace of a usurping dynasty was something sixteenth-century England was not prepared to tolerate. Northumberland and Lady Jane Grey

died. They were awe-inspiring reminders of the
new order under which king-makers were almost
certain to be brought to the block and usurpers
were bound to fail. Mary was accepted as a Tudor
who would carry on Tudor work.

Had she retained that position, English history
could not have been prevented from being very
different from what it was. She chose, however,
to hazard her crown on behalf of the Papacy.
She insisted on a marriage with Philip of Spain.
Her first parliament, recognizing the need for a
provision with regard to the succession, petitioned
her to marry an Englishman, but she rejected the
suggestion. On October 1553 she allowed it to
be known that she was prepared to marry Philip,
son of the Emperor Charles V.

Spain had already been an ominous name in
English history, and Mary's subjects might well
begin to fancy they could see on the horizon signs
of history that would repeat itself. A Spanish
marriage had been the cause of half the troubles
of the period. What was to be expected of the
new alliance ? The situation was far worse than
it had been earlier. The importation of a king
consort was in itself a matter full of danger. So
much so, that the signature of the marriage treaty
in January 1556 was almost immediately followed
by a rising in Devonshire under Sir Peter Carew,
and by the much more dangerous outburst headed
by Sir Thomas Wyatt in Kent in the following
March. Although Wyatt's rising failed, its importance was great. It is true that the cause of
the failure was very largely the lack of support

experienced by the rebels, and on the surface it would appear as though this were an indication of Mary's strength. In reality the facts were otherwise. The mere existence of the rebellion was an ominous sign of future events. There was, as yet, not enough active opposition in the country to ensure success for an insurrection, but there was much unrest lurking unseen. Every step in Mary's policy was calculated to increase it. Wyatt's rebellion is the sign that the enthusiasm of the early years of the reign had already begun to fade.

The protests of Englishmen were the product of sound common sense. Men were fully alive to the dangers in store for their country. An alliance with Spain meant an alliance with the power that was rapidly becoming dominant in Europe. Since 1519, when Charles V. had acquired the Empire, his efforts had been concentrated upon an increase of power in Europe. He had not been unsuccessful. It was not to be expected that Englishmen should feel easy at the prospects. Philip would one day rule in Charles's place. It was not in the nature of things that he intended to relinquish his prospects for the sake of becoming a puppet by the side of Mary's throne. The marriage was the most serious threat to English insularity that had been made for generations, since it meant the possible end of England's existence as an independent country. In such an eventuality, the work of Henry VII. would all have been done in vain, and the country which owed its prosperity to the studied policy whereby its kings had kept it out of European affairs would soon become a small dependency of the Spanish Empire, ruled over by a foreigner, valued only as a field of exploitation for the purposes of Spanish policy, and lost in the tremendous possessions of Spain. That such a result was at least possible there could be little doubt in the minds of many of Mary's subjects. To imagine that England would benefit by being thus swallowed up by Spain was not to be dreamed. There could be no commercial advantages to be gained, for there was no intention of allowing England to share in the markets of the New World, and the political disadvantages of the new situation were obvious. Little wonder, then, that popular hostility to the marriage was great. Wyatt's rebellion expressed what many Englishmen were thinking, even though they were not as yet prepared to act their thoughts by joining that demonstration.

It would have required much greater manifestations than the rebellion to turn Mary from her purpose. The marriage treaty was not likely to be cancelled because her subjects saw impending political and commercial disadvantages. One thing, however, parliament did succeed in obtaining. A successful attempt was made to safeguard English interests by the act of April 1554, which vested the royal power in the queen as fully as it had been vested in kings of England. The statute is of importance, because it was a definite declaration of the principle that a woman could occupy the English throne ; but it was something more than an expression of a principle with regard to the succession. It was an attempt to look after English interests in the face of the Spanish marriage and its inevitable consequences. It was the English answer to the Habsburg menace.

That it would be enough no one would say. Philip and Mary reigned together after the marriage, and it would have passed human ingenuity to devise a complete system of checks which would keep Philip's influence out of English affairs. The feeling rapidly grew that the foreigner had entered England in order to use its resources for the fulfilment of Spanish aims. Popular support veered away from Mary. The religious policy began a feeling of estrangement. When persecution came it was taken as an indication of Spanish methods, and these various factors combined to rob Mary of the sympathy of her subjects.

It cannot be said that the immediate sequence of foreign policy did much to allay popular suspicion. Philip had little interest in English affairs. By 1556 he had taken upon himself responsibilities his father was relinquishing in order to go into his seclusion. They were responsibilities which soon involved him in the meshes of European diplomacy. It was not long before he was in difficulties. The chief of these was a problem reacting upon English politics. The complications of Spanish policy in Italy brought Philip into controversy with a dangerous antagonist in the person of Pope Paul IV., who ascended the papal throne in 1555. His objections to Spanish interference in Italy made him violently hostile to Philip, whom he excommunicated. Playing on European rivalries, he won the support of France, and by January 1557 the quarrel between him and Philip had grown into a general European conflict in which the Papacy and France faced Spain, Savoy, and Tuscany.

Mary was in an impossible position. The two influences which can best be described as the two guiding stars in her life were at war. Which was she to support ? On the one hand, her obligation as a wife made it impossible for her to do other than support Philip, even if it meant going to war. On the other hand, her spiritual welfare made it worse than treason to deny her spiritual father. The dilemma was solved for the wretched woman by an external factor. Thomas Stafford, the grandson of that Duke of Buckingham whom Henry VIII. put to death, developed a mad scheme—which France very naturally supported —for capturing Mary's throne. As a conspiracy it was a failure, which ended in his execution. As a decisive influence in foreign policy, it ended in forcing Mary to take her husband's side. By June 1557 England was at war with France. The unpreparedness of England for war, and the gross incompetence with which the campaign was carried out, need not detain us. One vital result followed. By January 1558 the French were in Calais, and the last English territory on the continent was lost.

The loss of Calais was one of the enduring benefits Mary gave to her country. She did not know it, neither did her people. They regarded the loss as a bitter humiliation, and the failure to recapture it as a mark of the depths to which the country was sinking under her rule. It is easier to be tolerant in the light of history. Calais was a relic of an age that was passing away. It was an encumbrance. Its upkeep was expensive in men and money. It was a constant source of anxiety owing to its position in another country. It was the subject of never-ceasing trouble between England and France. Its strategic value as a key to France meant that it was a temptation to attacks on that country, and its continued retention could only have led to further troubles. On the other hand, the value placed upon it by contemporaries was exaggerated. The thought of it as a staple town was what lingered in their minds. But it must be remembered that mediæval trading methods were passing away. With their passing, with the growth of the new trade-routes and the new methods, the commercial significance was withering. England would survive its loss, and, apart from the disgraceful way in which it was lost, its fall in 1558 was productive of no evil results for this country.

There will always be two opinions of the value of the work which Mary strove to do. It is a topic which must be approached in the light of all that has already been said about the political and religious problems of the age. But even those most bitterly opposed to Mary's work may be expected to spare a tribute to the woman herself and to the man who served her to the end. Mary

Tudor and cardinal Pole fought for what they honestly believed to be the truth, and in their fight there was none of the self-seeking which mars so much of the story we have tried to tell. They were ranged on the side of a losing cause, and it is easy to belittle the sacrifices they made. Maybe there would be nothing to attract if the cause they were supporting had emerged triumphant. It is not the virtues of that cause which command respect, but their own idealism, the honesty of their intentions, the pathos of their lives. Unchivalrous, intolerant indeed, is the spirit that cannot weigh against the awful mistakes they made the fervour—albeit the futility—of their methods and their aims.

After Calais there were not to be many more mistakes. On November 17, 1558, the last melancholy moments of Mary's ill-starred reign were passing swiftly away. In the small hours the weary, heart-broken woman lay dying. At eight in the morning parliament was assembled and heard the news that she was dead. As the bells of Westminster rang out the message to the world, cardinal Pole at Lambeth, found faithful even unto death, was relinquishing his task. By eventide he had gone to join his queen.

The message of the bells spread through London and into the country-side beyond. It reached Hatfield, where it was heard by a young woman of twenty-five, the daughter of Henry VIII. and Anne Boleyn. She prepared to enter into her heritage. The Marian reaction was spent.

In Mary's reign it is impossible to forget at any moment the personal tragedy that was being played. When all has been said and done, when all the great forces have been taken into consideration, when the many problems have all been examined, there still remains the pathetic figure of that queen. It would be wrong to leave the study of her reign without attempting to appreciate the sombre character upon the forefront of the stage.

The attempt must be made sympathetically, for Mary Tudor is the most pathetic figure in all our history. Hers was the tragedy of a bountiful giver whose gifts, though prodigal, were never wholly adequate. It is only necessary to recall the greatest of her sacrifices to realize that melancholy truth. To Philip, when he wooed her, she gave her heart. But she could not give him either youth or beauty. To the same cold, imperious prince, when he had married her, she gave a kingdom—all that she possessed. But she could not give him the son for whom she yearned. To Mother Church, whose loyal child she ever strove to be, she gave again supremacy over England. But she could not restore the wealth of which the Church had been despoiled or the loyal devotion of a people alienated from the Faith. And as though all this were not enough, there was one more bitterness in the cup of sorrows this lonely woman had to drain. She had given so lavishly of all she had, that when her subjects sought from her what they could rightly claim, she had nothing more to give—nothing save the memory of her own name after she had stained it with the blood of men and women whom they loved. Yet here was the gift that was of greater consequence than all the rest. For once again in human history the blood of the martyrs was to be the seed of the Church.

.   .   .   .

The reader who has followed this brief sketch of the fortunes of England under the Tudor dynasty will have drawn his own conclusions about the quality of what was done in these crowded years. Whatever may be his feelings towards the men and movements responsible for the changes taking place, he is not likely to have missed their meaning. England had been ruthlessly taken in hand by strong men, and the result of their deeds was a new method of government that, for lack of a better phrase, we have called the Tudor despotism. The experiments initiated by these new rulers inflicted much suffering, and much they did was grievous error. Those in charge were not as yet masters of the complicated machinery they had brought into being. They were more conscious of their own power than they were of their responsibilities, and the experience they were acquiring was paid for by their subjects. Yet, after more than seventy years of Tudor experiment, the machine was at last ready for use. It needed only the masterful control of the expert to put it to the test. The moment for that was at hand. England was to find in Queen Elizabeth a ruler equipped with that technique of government which could transform the menace of a Tudor despotism into the achievement of an Elizabethan Age.

APPENDICES

APPENDIX I

SOME LANDMARKS, 1485–1558

Note.—The table on the following pages is an arbitrary arrangement of some of the main dates and facts which have to be remembered in studying this period. It does not attempt to indicate general movements (*e.g.* economic movements like that of Enclosure), and is only likely to be of use to those who wish to be reminded of some of the important facts which illustrate some of the points made in preceding pages.

YEAR	POLITICAL.	CONSTITUTIONAL.	ECCLESIASTICAL.	GENERAL CULTURE.	SOCIAL AND ECONOMIC.
1485.	Battle of Bosworth. Coronation. Truce with France.	Parliament (Nov. 7). 1. Recognition of Henry's title. 2. Grant of Tonnage and Poundage. 3. Resumption of Crown Lands. 4. Repeal of Attainders. 5. Acts of Attainder.	Act for Bishops to punish Clergy for evil living.		Navigation Act.
1486.	Henry married Elizabeth of York. Rebellion of Lovell and Stafford. Birth of Prince Arthur.		Papal Dispensation for Royal Marriage.		Act against Usury.
1487.	Lambert Simnel's Rebellion. Battle of Stoke.	Parliament (Nov.). The "Star Chamber" Act.	Papal Bull against Sanctuary.		
1488.	Woodville's Expedition to Brittany. Death of Francis, Duke of Brittany. Negotiations with Spain.			Linacre goes to Italy. Studies under Politian.	
1489.	Treaty of Medina del Campo.	Parliament (Jan. 13). Act for due execution of their commissions by J.P.'s.	Act taking away Benefit of Clergy from certain persons.		Act against the pulling down of towns.
1490.	Commercial Treaty with Denmark.			Grocyn returns from Italy. Lectures at Oxford.	
1491.	Anne of Brittany marries Charles VIII. Birth of Henry VIII.	Parliament (Oct. 17).			Act regulating Weights and Measures.
1492.	Perkin Warbeck at Cork. Invasion of France.				
1493.	Peace of Etaples.	Records of Court of Requests begin.		Thomas More at Oxford	

1494.	Perkin Warbeck in Netherlands. Commercial Relations with Netherlands broken off.				Act against Vagabonds and Beggars. Act for Weights and Measures. Act against Usury.
1495.	Perkin Warbeck off Deal (July). Perkin Warbeck in Scotland (Nov.).	Parliament (Oct. 14). Legislation for Law and Order. 1. Act against Riots and Unlawful Assemblies. 2. Act against Sheriffs. 3. Act against Perjury. 4. Act against Juries giving False Verdicts. 5. Act against Unlawful Maintenances. 6. Act giving poor right to sue in *forma pauperis*. 7. Statute of Treason.			
1496.	Henry joins the Holy League. The Magnus Intercursus.		Act further limiting Benefit of Clergy.	Colet returns from Italy. Lectures at Oxford. Thomas More studies Law at Lincoln's Inn.	Licence to Cabot.
1497.	The Cornish Rising. Warbeck captured.				
1498.			Henry refuses to join Crusade.	Grocyn lectures at Oxford. Erasmus at Oxford. Erasmus's *Adagia* published. Erasmus's *Enchiridion*.	
1499.	Execution of the Earl of Warwick, and Warbeck. De la Pole's Plot.				
1500.					
1501.	Prince Arthur marries Catherine of Aragon.				
1502.	Marriage of Margaret Tudor to James IV. Death of Prince Arthur.				

YEAR	POLITICAL.	CONSTITUTIONAL.	ECCLESIASTICAL.	GENERAL CULTURE.	SOCIAL AND ECONOMIC.
1503.	Death of Queen. Henry made Prince of Wales.			Lady Margaret founds Professorships at Oxford and Cambridge.	
1504.	Death of Queen Isabella of Spain.	Parliament (Jan. 25). Act to repress Riots. Act against Liveries.	Papal Dispensation for marriage of Henry and Catherine.	More lectures on St. Augustine's *City of God.* More studies Pico della Mirandola. Colet made Dean of St. Paul's.	Act against Vagabonds.
1505.	Prince Henry denounces Marriage Contract.			Erasmus in England.	
1506.	Archduke Philip in England. The Malus Intercursus.				
1507.	Henry negotiates for marriage with Joanna of Castile.				
1509.	Death of Henry VII. Henry VIII. marries Catherine.	Empson and Dudley executed.			
1510.		Parliament (Jan. 21). New Acts for Law and Order.			Act against Costly Apparel.
1511.	Wolsey in the King's Council. Preparations for War.			Colet founds St. Paul's School.	
1512.	Expedition to help Spain.		Colet attacks abuses in the Church in Convocation Sermon.	Erasmus at Cambridge. Published *Praise of Folly.*	
1513.	Invasion of France; Battle of the Spurs; Terouenne; Tournai. Battle of Flodden.		Benefit of Clergy limited.	Erasmus visits Walsingham. Leaves Cambridge.	
1514.	Peace with France. Louis XII. marries Mary Tudor.	Parliament (Jan.).	Richard Hunne's Case.		

				Erasmus in England.	
1515.	Wolsey becomes Cardinal and Lord Chancellor. Accession of Francis I.	Parliament. Act forbidding 'members to leave before end of Parliament.	Standish's dispute about Benefit of Clergy.		Act against Enclosures. Act against Costly Apparel.
1516.				More's *Utopia*. Erasmus's *New Testament*.	
1517.	Treaty of Universal Peace.	Court of Requests fixed at Whitehall.	Protestant party at Cambridge. Wolsey made Papal Legate.		May Day Riot.
1518.				More enters king's service.	Commission on Enclosures.
1519.	Charles V. elected Emperor.		Luther's Theses against Church.	Death of Colet.	
1520.	Field of Cloth of Gold.				
1521.	Wolsey joins Charles V. Death of Pope Leo X.		Henry VIII. writes Book against Luther.		
1522.	Election of Adrian VI. War with France.				
1523.	Death of Adrian VI.	Parliament. Opposition to War Taxation. Wolsey in conflict.			
1524.			Wolsey gets papal permission for his colleges.		
1525.	Battle of Pavia. Truce with France.				
1527.	Sack of Rome by Charles V. Collusive suit to get rid of Catherine of Aragon.				
1528.			Decretal Commission *re* divorce.		
1529.	Legatine Court sits to discuss divorce. Cranmer suggests appeal to Universities.	Parliament (Nov.).	Attack on some abuses: 1. Probate Act. 2. Mortuaries Act. 3. Pluralities Act.	Simon Fish's *Supplication of Beggars*. Attack on Church. More's *Supplication of Souls* answers Fish.	

YEAR	POLITICAL.	CONSTITUTIONAL.	ECCLESIASTICAL.	GENERAL CULTURE.	SOCIAL AND ECONOMIC.
1529.	Praemunire against Wolsey, who surrenders Great Seal. More becomes Lord Chancellor.		Clergy under Praemunire. King's pardon to: (1) Clergy of Canterbury; (2) Laity.	Sir Thomas Elyot's *Governour* published.	Act concerning Beggars.
1530.	Death of Wolsey.				
1531.	Rise of Cromwell.				
1532.	More resigns Chancellorship.		Statutes *re* Church: 1. Benefit of Clergy. 2. Restraint of Annates. Pardon to Clergy of York. Cranmer Archbishop of Canterbury. Act in Restraint of Appeals.		
1533.	Henry VIII. marries Anne Boleyn. Cranmer holds court at Dunstable and declares marriage of Henry and Catherine void. Henry appeals from Pope to General Council. Birth of Elizabeth.				
1534.	Elizabeth Barton's case. More and Fisher implicated.	1st Act for the Succession. Act of Supremacy. 2nd Act for the Succession. Treason Act.	Submission of the Clergy. Act in Restraint of Appeals. Act in Restraint of Annates. Act in Restraint of Peter's Pence. Benefit of Clergy. Visitation of Monasteries begins. Henry Head of Church in England. Cromwell as Vicar-General.		
1535.	Execution of Fisher and More.			Thomas Starkey's *England under Henry VIII.* Coverdale translating the *Bible.*	

1536.	Death of Catherine. Execution of Anne Boleyn.	Incorporation of Wales. Court of Augmentations set up.	1st Act for Dissolution of Monasteries. The Ten Articles.	Coverdale's *Bible* licensed.	Act *re* Beggars.
1537.	Henry marries Jane Seymour. Birth of Prince Edward. Death of Jane Seymour. Pilgrimage of Grace.	Council of North definitely organized.			
1538.	Henry VIII. excommunicated.		Injunctions.		
1539.	Henry marries Anne of Cleves.	Act of Proclamations.	2nd Act for Dissolution of Monasteries. The Six Articles.	The *Great Bible* published.	
1540.	Cromwell sent to Tower. King's marriage declared void. Henry marries Catherine Howard. Execution of Cromwell.	Parliament. Court of First Fruits and Tenths. Court of Wards and Liveries.			
1542. 1543.	Catherine Howard executed. Ultimatum to France. Henry marries Catherine Parr.	Court of Surveyors. Court of Marches of Wales on statutory basis. Succession Act.	The King's Book.		
1546.	Execution of Anne Askewe. Norfolk and Surrey sent to Tower.			Trinity College, Cambridge, founded by Henry VIII.	
1547.	Death of Henry VIII. Accession of Edward VI. Battle of Pinkie.	Appointment of Somerset as Protector. Parliament (Nov.). Repeal of Treason Laws.	Repeal of Heresy Laws. Dissolution of Chantries.	Peter Martyr at Oxford.	Attack on Gilds.
1548.					
1549.	Risings against Uniformity. War with France. Somerset falls, and Northumberland takes his place.	New Treason Laws.	Foreign Reformers come to England. 1st Act of Uniformity. 1st Book of Common Prayer. Marriage of Priests Legalized. Act against Superstitious Books and Images. The Ordinal.		Ket's Rebellion. Agitation against Enclosures.
1550.	Somerset released from Tower. Peace with France.				

YEAR	POLITICAL.	CONSTITUTIONAL.	ECCLESIASTICAL.	GENERAL CULTURE.	SOCIAL AND ECONOMIC.
1551.	Somerset v. Northumberland. Arrest and trial of Somerset.				Debasement of Coinage.
1552.	Execution of Somerset.	Parliament. Statute of Treason.	2nd Act of Uniformity. 2nd Book of Common Prayer. Forty-two Articles. Attempted reform of Common Law.		
1553.	Death of Edward VI. Northumberland and Lady Jane Grey. Success of Mary. Execution of Northumberland. Accession of Mary.	Statute of Treason. Parliament. Repeal of Treason Laws.	Arrest of Cranmer, Latimer, Hooper, Coverdale. Flight of Foreign Reformers. 1st Statute of Repeal. Injunctions.		
1554.	Wyatt's Rebellion. Marriage of Philip and Mary. Return of Pole.	Parliament. 3rd Parliament.	Revival of Heresy Laws. Parliament petitions for Reconciliation with Rome. Pole absolves England.	Antonio Moro, Flemish artist, in England.	Risings in Midlands and West.
1555.		Treason Law. 4th Parliament.	Repeal of Henry VIII.'s anti-papal Legislation. Religious persecution.		
1556. 1557.	Stafford's Invasion. War with France.				
1558.	Loss of Calais. Death of Mary. Death of Pole.	Parliament.	Execution of Cranmer.		

APPENDIX II

A NOTE ON READING

THIS sketch of early Tudor England has been written for those to whom that period of our history is unfamiliar ground, and if it succeeds in supplying some such general impression as is gained from a first prospect of an unknown landscape it will have achieved its purpose. At the same time it is to be hoped that like such a first glimpse of new country-side it will also be an incentive to exploration. Your experienced traveller is he who knows that it is only when he has descended to the plain and walked on unfamiliar fields and sought out hidden bypaths that he will learn the secrets a landscape hides from view. So, too, the reader must explore if he would know the land this sketch has only roughly mapped.

He will find the task a pleasing one, for the period is rich in historical literature of high quality, and the men and movements with which it deals have singular attractions. He will find also that his task is an exacting one. The books are many, the variety of subjects dealt with is great. The novice runs some risk of bewilderment if he attempts to choose his way without a guide. Perhaps it will be permitted for one aware of the deficiencies of this sketch in a way not equalled by its most severe critic, to reduce its deficiencies by some words of guidance in the choice of method to be used in filling in what it omits.

Men have held that the history of a country is the biography of its great men. If that be true, then surely the history of Tudor England can be adequately studied. There was no lack of important personages, and they have had their biographers. If we take G. Temperley, *Henry VII.*, A. F. Pollard, *Cardinal Wolsey* and his *Henry VIII.*, P. Friedmann, *Anne Boleyn*, R. B. Merriman, *Life and Letters of Thomas Cromwell*, A. F. Pollard, *Thomas Cranmer* and his *England under Protector Somerset*, J. A. Muller, *Stephen Gardiner and the Tudor Reaction*, J. M. Stone, *Mary I.*, and M. Haile, *Cardinal Pole*, we shall be supplied with a chain of biographies linking together the years from 1485 to 1558. And in *The Great Tudors*, edited by Katharine Garvin, will be found a set of short biographical essays by various authors which include most of the leading characters of the period. Such books will yield much general information, but they will be read in vain unless they give rise to questions which challenge the accuracy of the statement that all history is biography. For they ought to open on to problems which they do not adequately solve, and thus they should give point to Lord Acton's advice that in history the study of problems is preferable to the study of periods. Such a thought opens the way to historical books of another kind. Let us examine some of the possibilities of study suggested by this advice.

Little reading is needed to bring the reader into touch with the Tudor government, and he will soon be calling for books to which he can turn for help in understanding its nature and development. In Kenneth Pickthorn, *Early Tudor Government* (2 vols.), he will find a large scale attempt at a summary of recent work on the subject, while in W. S. Holdsworth, *History of English Law* (Vols. IV. and V.), he has at hand a lawyer's interpretation of the Tudor constitution, and in J. R. Tanner, *Tudor Constitutional Documents*, he will be provided not merely with summaries of modern research work on special aspects of the subject, but also with the essential documentary evidence on which many of these books must necessarily be based. An appetite unsatisfied by these works has to be treated very seriously, and is a case for the expert. Specialists have done much in many branches of constitutional history, but it would not be possible to list all their works here. As specimens of the problems dealt with in such monographs mention may be made of A. F. Pollard, *Evolution of Parliament*, and his articles on *The Council, Star Chamber and Privy Council under the Tudors* (*English Historical Review*, XXXVII.), Lord E. Percy, *Privy Council under the Tudors*, J. F. Baldwin, *King's Council in the Middle Ages*, C. Scofield, *Court of Star Chamber*, C. A. J. Skeel, *Council of the Marches in Wales*, W. Llewellyn Williams, *The Making of Modern Wales*, R. Reid, *Council of the North*, I. S. Leadam, *Select Cases in the Court of Star Chamber* and *Select Cases in the Court of Requests*, F. C. Dietz, *English Government Finance*, and the set of special essays in *Tudor Studies* (edited by R. W. Seton Watson). And, as an interpretation of the thought which lay behind much of the political activity mention must be made of J. W. Allen's profoundly wise *History of Political Thought in the Sixteenth Century*. Such works are not to be rushed at incautiously. This list contains a miscellaneous—albeit an important—assortment of the kind of work that is being done, but which of these books are to be tasted, which swallowed, which chewed, which skipped, and which read by deputy will best be discovered by the reader who knows his own mind.

Let us take another problem. The religious issues of this period lead to different fields, but the method to be adopted in pursuing them remains the same. For a general survey the work of G. Constant, *The English Reformation*: *The Anglican Schism*, may be recommended. To understand the questions of doctrine and morality involved, a knowledge of the state of the Church on the eve of the Reformation is essential. Books like F. A. Gasquet, *England on the Eve of the*

Reformation and *Henry VIII. and the Dissolution of the Monasteries*, will give a favourable view of the English Church. G. Perry, *Reformation in England*, J. Gairdner, *History of the English Church*, and R. W. Dixon, *History of the English Church*, supply material for a modification of this view. The article on ecclesiastical history by Miss E. J. Davis in the *Victoria County History, London* (Vol. I.), might well be made the starting-point of any intensive study of this aspect of Tudor history. Doctrinal questions may be studied in C. H. Smyth, *Cranmer and the Reformation under Edward VI.*, F. A. Gasquet and E. Bishop, *Edward VI. and the Book of Common Prayer*, F. Procter and W. H. Frere, *A New History of the Book of Common Prayer*.

The intellectual life of the times is closely connected with religious history and calls for an understanding of the renaissance movement. The most necessary books are L. Einstein, *Italian Renaissance in England*, J. H. Lupton, *Life of Colet*, E. M. G. Routh, *Sir Thomas More*, T. E. Bridgett, *Life of More*, F. Seebohm, *Oxford Reformers*, A. W. Reed, *Early Tudor Drama*, and A. F. Leach, *English Schools at the Reformation*. A sentence must be spared to commend the scholarship, wit, and profound common sense of the *Life of Thomas More*, by Professor R. W. Chambers (1935), a work which should be read by all who seek to understand this aspect of Tudor history.

Tudor men were not always dealing with problems of government and religion. Like us they, too, had their social and economic difficulties, and many readers—attracted by the modern fashion in historical study—will consider the contributions this period made to the social and economic development of England more important than these other aspects we have mentioned. They will find essential such works as E. Lipson, *The Economic History of England*, W. Cunningham, *Growth of English Industry and Commerce*, E. P. Cheyney, *Social Changes in England in the Sixteenth*

Century, R. H. Tawney, *Agrarian Problem in the Sixteenth Century* and *Religion and the Rise of Capitalism,* A. Savine, *Dissolution of the Monasteries,* G. Unwin, *Industrial Organization in the Sixteenth and Seventeenth Centuries,* and G. Prothero, *English Farming Past and Present.*

Thus, suggestions for the study of problems in Tudor history might be made almost indefinitely ; but it will be more useful to conclude this note with an indication of the method which ought to be applied to any branch of study. Whatever may be the problem under discussion, it should first be approached by way of the *Political History of England* (Vols. IV. and V.). Here will be found admirable bibliographies which provide—in conjunction with those to be found in the *Cambridge Modern History* (Vols. I. and II.)—a direct guide to special subjects. For the specialist reader the most recent and the fullest bibliography is Conyers Read, *Bibliography of British History, Tudor Period, 1485–1603.* These lists may be brought up to date by using the annual surveys of historical writing provided in the *Bulletin of Historical Literature,* published by the Historical Association. If biographical material is needed, recourse should be had to the *Dictionary of National Biography.* Perhaps this is the place to remind the reader that Froude's *History of England* still remains an important narrative history of the period. Despite all the criticisms levelled against the work it is still useful, and certainly more of a literary delight than most of the productions of its most severe critics.

When the reader has exhausted the monographs in the above-mentioned bibliographies there will still be work to do. He will not know the Tudor period if he is content to read what modern historians have to say about it. The spirit of an age is only to be appreciated by contact with the thought of the age. A general idea of contemporary literature may be gleaned from such collections as A. F. Pollard, *Sources for the Reign of*

Henry VII., C. H. Williams, *England under the Early Tudors*, J. R. Tanner, *Tudor Constitutional Documents*, and R. H. Tawney and E. Power, *Tudor Economic Documents*. There are classics, too, that must be read. Of these it must be sufficient to mention More's *Utopia*, Roper's *Life of More*, Cavendish's *Life of Wolsey*, Latimer's *Sermons*, Sir Thomas Elyot's *Boke of the Governour*, which are all obtainable in cheap editions, while P. S. Allen, *Selections from Erasmus*, forms an introduction to his splendid edition of that writer's letters.

Behind such materials loom the enormous mass of state papers and official records of diverse kinds which all have to be known before the available material is exhausted. But by the time the reader has recognized the importance of such sources he will be far beyond the help of such a cursory list as this, and will be able and anxious to ferret them out for himself.

INDEX

ANNE, of Beaujeu, 39 ; of Brittany, 40, 262 ; of Cleves, 149, 150, 168, 267.
Aquitaine, 45.
Aragon, Ferdinand of, *see* Spain.
Arthur, Prince of Wales, 43, 46, 262, 263.
Articles, the Ten, 142 ; the Six, 143.
Aske, Robert, 161.
Askewe, Anne, 267.
Assertio Septem Sacramentorum, 141.
Audley, Sir Thomas, Lord Chancellor, 164.

BAINBRIDGE, Christopher, Cardinal Archbishop of York, 86.
Barton, Elizabeth, 150, 163, 266.
Bible, editions of, 144, 267 ; use of enforced, 223.
Bishops, appointment of, 69, 225.
Boleyn, Anne, 115, 125, 127, 128, 138, 148, 149, 163, 266, 267.
Bosworth, Battle of, 1–4, 9, 262.
Bray, Reginald, 22.
Bristol, merchants of, 52.
Brittany, 39, 40, 41.
Bucer, Martin, 209, 213, 229.

CABOT, John, 52, 263.
Calais, 85, 256, 257, 268.
Campo, Medina del, 44, 262.
Canon Law, Reform of, 228.
Canterbury, 63, 157.
Captivity, the Babylonish, 31.
Carew, Sir Peter, 252.
Casale, Sir Gregory, 125.
Castile, Isabella of, 37, 44, 264 ; Joanna of, 48, 264.
Catherine of Aragon, 44, 46, 47, 77, 109, 114, 122, 124–126, 128, 163, 265, 267.
Cavendish, quotations from, 96–98, 134.
Cerdagne, 44, 45.
Chantries, dissolution of, 225, 267.
Chapuys, Eustace, 153.

Charles V., *see* Spain.
Charles VIII., *see* France.
Cheyney, Sir John, 22.
Christ Church College, 104.
Church, the, in England, 56–67, 136, 138, 139 ; doctrine in, 141–143 ; privileges of, 59, 67, 69, 116, 118, 133, 137 ; property of, 65, 155, 156, 248 ; relations with State, 54, 65, 66, 112, 119, 133–135, 137–138, 159–160, 211–212, 249.
Clergy, benefit of, 70, 118, 139, 262–265 ; celibacy of, 228 ; non-residence of, 65, 118 ; pardon of, 119.
Cloth of Gold, Field of, 108.
Coinage, debasement of, 200, 239, 268.
Colet, John, 77, 78, 80, 263–265.
Colleges, foundation of, 155.
Colloquies, the, of Erasmus, 63.
Columbus, 51.
Commerce, Henry VII. and, 49–51.
Conciliar Movement, the, 31.
Constantinople, 34, 36.
Conway, Sir Hugh, 22.
Council, the : Judicial powers of, 17, 171, 173 ; Parliament and, 180 ; personnel of, 22 ; value of to Tudors, 171–172, 174, 180, 184 ; Henry VII. and, 22 ; Henry VIII. and, 172, 173, 189–190 ; Edward VI. and, 189–190, 228.
Council of the Marches (Wales), 166, 173, 267 ; of the North, 173, 267 ; of the West, 174.
Counter-reformation, the English, 241.
Courts : of Arches, 103 ; Audience, 103 ; Augmentations, 174, 267 ; Common Law, 15, 18 ; Requests, 94, 173, 262 ; Star Chamber, 17–20, 94, 98, 173 ; Surveyors, 174, 267 ; Wards and Liveries, 174, 267.

277

INDEX

INDEX

Isabella of Castile, *see* Castile.
Italy, 32, 36, 72, 108.

JOANNA OF CASTILE, *see* Castile.
Jury System, the, 11, 16.

KATHERINE OF ARAGON, *see* Catherine.

LASCO, John a, 213.
Latimer, Hugh, 248, 250, 268.
Lawlessness, 11, 14, 15, 17, 23, 94.
Learning, the New, *see* Renaissance.
Lee, Roland, 166.
Legal procedure, reform of, 13, 15, 16.
Linacre, Thomas, 72, 77, 262.
Litany, 221.
Livery, 11, 14, 19, 200.
Loans, forced, 25.
Lollardy, 71, 140, 155.
Louis XI., XII., *see* France.
Luther, Martin, 74, 214, 215, 222, 265.

MACHIAVELLI, 152.
Maintenance, 14, 17, 19, 200.
Margaret, of Burgundy, 7, 42 ; of Savoy, 48 ; Tudor, 155, 263, 264.
Marignano, Battle of, 107.
Martyr, Peter, 209, 213, 218, 229, 267.
Martyrs, Tombs of, 63.
Mary, Queen, 171, 187, 196, 232, 237 ; importance of reign of, 232, 237, 252 ; character of, 236 ; criticism of, 257–260 ; religious policy of, 241, 245, 250 ; Spanish policy of, 242, 244, 251, 252.
Mary Tudor, 107.
Minority, Royal, significance of, 184, 188, 190.
Mirandola, Pico della, 78, 264.
Monarchy, new view of, 183.
Monasteries, condition of, 65, 158 ; dissolution of, 154–160, 161, 226, 267.
Monasticism, 61.
More, Sir Thomas, 73, 74, 77, 78, 79, 150, 162, 163, 266 ; Alice, 164.
Moro, Antonio, 268.
Mountjoy, William, Lord, 77.
Mousehold Heath, 203.

NANFAN, Sir Richard, 85.
Nationalism, growth of, 33, 35.

Nobles, Henry VII. and, 16.
Northumberland, Duke of, 191, 267, 268 ; Edward VI. and, 194 ; religious policy of, 219–220 ; criticism of, 194–196, 231, 251.

PAPACY, the, temporal aims of, 32, 132 ; Renaissance and, 32 ; Empire and, 31, 33, 107, 109 ; Henry VII. and, 67 ; Henry VIII. and, 185.
Parliament : Henry VII. and, 3, 5, 99 ; Henry VIII. and, 178 ; Wolsey and, 99 ; Mary and, 239, 245, 254 ; and the Reformation, 116–123, 135, 138 ; and succession, 3, 254, 262 ; independence of, 136, 170, 172, 180, 181 ; sessions of, 180.
Parr, Catherine, 150, 267.
Pavia, Battle of, 108, 265.
Peace, Justices of, 16, 175, 206, 262.
Persecution, 248.
Peter's Pence, 121.
Philip, Archduke, 50, 264.
Philip II., *see* Spain.
Pilgrimage of Grace, 161, 203, 267.
Pinkie, Battle of, 193, 267.
Pole, Edmund de la, 7 ; Reginald, 245, 258, 268.
Poverty, problem of, 202–208.
Præmunire, 118, 266.
Prayer, Book of Common, 227.
Priories, alien, 155.
Proclamations, statutes of, 171, 182, 267.
Puebla, Roderigo de, 7.

REFORMATION : in Europe, 74, 75, 213, 215–218 ; in England, 17, 54*ff.* ; problems of, 54–55, 67, 114, 115, 123, 132, 135 ; insularity of, 75, 229 ; political aspect of, 140 ; doctrinal aspect of, 185, 211, 213.
Regency, Council of, 189.
Regent, dangers of, 190.
Renaissance : in Italy, 72 ; in England, 70, 71, 78 ; significance of, 71, 79.
Richard III., 1, 2, 5, 21, 39.
Rogers, Thorold, 201.
Rome, sack of, 109, 265.
Roses, Wars of, 10, 14, 22, 27, 49.
Roussillon, 44.

279

INDEX